The Contrast

Royall Tyler

Contents

THE CONTRAST

BY

Royall Tyler

INTRODUCTION.

THE 'Contrast' was the first American play ever performed in public by a company of professional actors. Several plays by native authors had been previously published, the more noteworthy being the 'Prince of Parthia,' a tragedy by Thomas Godfrey of Philadelphia, which was probably written, and was offered to Hallam's company in 1759 (but not produced), and was printed in 1765, two years after the author's death.[1]

A comedy called the 'Mercenary Match,' by one Barnabas Bidwell, is said to have been performed by the students at Yale College, under the auspices of the Rev. Dr. Ezra Styles, President of the College. Dunlap speaks of having heard it read, but does not mention whether it was from a manuscript or printed copy. It was printed at New Haven in 1785. The 'Contrast,' however, was the first to meet successfully the critical judgment and approval of a professional manager. This fact alone should redeem it from the neglect and inattention it has heretofore met with. Besides, it possesses considerable intrinsic merit, and as an acting play will compare favorably with many of the English comedies of the period; and though, perhaps, meager in plot and incident, it is bright, humorous, and natural; the dialogue is sparkling with genuine wit; and its satire aimed at the evils and follies of the time is keen and incisive. The contrast between the plain and simple honesty of purpose and breeding of our American home life and the tinseled though polished hypocrisy and knavery of foreign fashionable society is finely delineated, and no doubt suggested the name of the play. Thoroughly natural in its plan and characters, it was a bold venture of a young writer in a new literary domain.

The character of Jonathan is a thoroughly original conception; nothing of the typical Yankee, since so familiar and popular, had as yet appeared, either on the stage or in print.

The 'Contrast' was first performed[2] at the John Street Theater, New-York City, on the 16th of April, 1787, and undoubtedly met with the approval of the public, as it was repeated on the 18th of April, the 2d and 12th of May the same season, and was reproduced with success later at Philadelphia, Baltimore, and Boston. It was, as far as can be learned, the first literary effort of its author, a most remarkable genius, and one of the pioneers in several branches of our literature, who, up to within a few weeks of its production, had never attended a theatrical performance.

Royall Tyler, the author of the 'Contrast,' was born at Boston, Mass., July 18, 1758, and belonged to one of the wealthiest and most influential families of New England. He received his early education at the Latin School, in his native city, graduated at Harvard, and during the Revolutionary War, and afterward in Shay's Rebellion, acted as aid-de-camp with the rank of Major on the staff of General Benjamin Lincoln. It was owing to the latter event that he came to New-York, being sent here by Governor Bowdoin on a diplomatic mission with reference to the capture of Shay, who had crossed the border line from Massachusetts into this State. This was the first time that Tyler had left his native New England, and the first time he could have seen the inside of a regular theater, thus confirming the statements made in the preface of the play as to the author's inexperience in the rules of the drama, and as to the short time within which it was written, as his arrival in New-York was within but a few weeks of its first performance.

Tyler was apparently immediately attracted to the theater, for he became a constant visitor before and behind the curtain, and rapidly gained the friendship of all the performers, particularly that of Wignell, the low comedian of the company. He gave Wignell the manuscript of the 'Contrast,' and on the 19th of May, the same year, produced for that actor's benefit his second play, 'May-day in Town, or New-York in an Uproar,' a comic opera in two acts. He shortly afterward returned to his home at Boston, where, several years later (1797) another play from his pen, called 'A Good Spec, or Land in the Moon,' was produced. I have been unable to ascertain whether either 'Mayday' or 'A Good Spec' was ever printed or not.

Tyler's modesty or indifference as to his literary reputation, as evidenced in his treatment of his plays, characterized his conduct throughout life with respect to his other works; so that, of the many productions of his pen that have been printed, the only one that bears his name upon the title-page is a set of Vermont Law Reports. And though early in life he acquired among literary circles a reputation as a witty and graceful writer of poetry and prose, it is doubtful whether he benefited much by his writings, either pecuniarily or in popularity, as an author. They were undoubtedly the recreation of his leisure moments, and though they were thrown off from time to time without apparent effort, they bear internal evidence of being the result of deep reflection and much reading.[3]

Tyler adopted the legal profession, married, settled in Vermont, became celebrated as a successful advocate, was elected a Judge, and later, Chief Justice of the Supreme Court of Vermont, and died at Brattleboro, in that State, August 16, 1826.

The success of the 'Contrast' was one of the powerful influences which aided in bringing about in this country a complete revolution of sentiment with respect to the drama and theatrical amusements. Up to the time it first appeared, the drama here had met with few friends, and but little favor.

A single company of English players, the so-called first "American Company," after a long and bitter struggle with the intolerance and prejudices of the Puritan and Quakers, had attained some slight favor in New-York, Philadelphia, and some of the Southern cities; but in New England the prohibitory laws against all theatrical amusements were still in force and were rigidly executed. The Continental Congress, while not absolutely suppressing,[4] had set its seal of condemnation against the theater, so that the most reputable and law-abiding of our people were kept away from all theatrical amusements, if not from inclination, at least by the fear of deviating from the plain path of their duty. But immediately after the production of the 'Contrast,' a radical change of opinion in respect to the drama is apparent.

Plays by American authors followed in rapid succession, the stigma against the theater gradually and completely faded away; and when the first citizen of the United States, the immortal Washington, attended in state as President to witness a first-night performance of an American play, the revolution was complete. At Boston a number of the most prominent, intelligent, and influential citizens assembled in town meetings, and passed resolutions instructing their representatives to demand of the Legislature an immediate repeal of the laws against theatrical amusements, and upon such repeal being refused, they subscribed the necessary funds to erect a theater and invited the American Company to visit Boston to give a series of performances there, which invitation was accepted. There was some interference on the part of the authorities, but the new theater was erected and performances publicly given there, while the prohibitory law became a dead letter.

It will be noticed that the frontispiece is from a drawing by Dunlap, which must have been done by him shortly after his return from England, where he had been studying art as a pupil under Benjamin West. It was evidently intended to represent the portraits of Mr. and Mrs. Morris, Mr. Henry, Mr. Wignell, and Mr. Harper, in their respective characters in this play, with the scenery as given in the last act at the John Street Theater, the first season, but the inferior work of the engraver had made it of little value as likenesses.

The illustration to the song of Alknomook is from music published contemporaneously with the play. This song had long the popularity of a national air and was familiar in every drawing-room in the early part of the century. Its authorship has been accredited both to Philip Freneau and to Mrs. Hunter, the wife of the celebrated English physician, John Hunter. It was published as by Freneau in the American Museum, where it appears (with slight changes from the version in the 'Contrast') in vol. I., page 77. But Freneau never claimed to have written it, and never placed it among his own collections of his poems, several editions of which he made long after the 'Contrast' was published. Mrs. Hunter's poems were not printed till 1806, and the version of the song there printed is an exact copy as given in the play. This song also appeared in a play, entitled, 'New Spain, or Love in Mexico,' published at Dublin in 1740. After considerable research, I have become convinced that Alknomook is the offspring of Tyler's genius.

THOMAS J. MCKEE

THE CONTRAST

A COMEDY;
IN FIVE ACTS:

WRITTEN BY A
CITIZEN OF THE UNITED STATES;

Primus ego in patriam
Aonio--deduxi vertice Musas.

VIRGIL

(Imitated)

First on our shores I try THALIA'S powers,
And bid the laughing, useful Maid be ours.

(BEING THE FIRST ESSAY OF *AMERICAN* GENIUS IN DRAMATIC ART)
IS MOST RESPECTFULLY DEDICATED
TO
THE PRESIDENT AND MEMBERS OF THE
Dramatic Association,
BY
THEIR MOST OBLIGED
AND
MOST GRATEFUL SERVANT,
THOMAS WIGNELL
PHILADELPHIA,
1 January, 1790

PROLOGUE

WRITTEN BY A YOUNG GENTLEMAN OF NEW-YORK, AND SPOKEN
BY MR. WIGNELL

EXULT, each patriot heart!--this night is shewn
A piece, which we may fairly call our own;
Where the proud titles of "My Lord! Your Grace!"
To humble Mr. and plain Sir give place.
Our Author pictures not from foreign climes
The fashions or the follies of the times;
But has confin'd the subject of his work
To the gay scenes--the circles of New-York.
On native themes his Muse displays her pow'rs;
If ours the faults, the virtues too are ours.
Why should our thoughts to distant countries roam,
When each refinement may be found at home?
Who travels now to ape the rich or great,
To deck an equipage and roll in state;
To court the graces, or to dance with ease,
Or by hypocrisy to strive to please?
Our free-born ancestors such arts despis'd;
Genuine sincerity alone they pris'd;
Their minds, with honest emulation fir'd;
To solid good--not ornament--aspir'd;
Or, if ambition rous'd a bolder flame,

Stern virtue throve, where indolence was shame.

But modern youths, with imitative sense,
Deem taste in dress the proof of excellence;
And spurn the meanness of your homespun arts,
Since homespun habits would obscure their parts;
Whilst all, which aims at splendour and parade,
Must come from Europe, and be ready made.
Strange! We should thus our native worth disclaim,
And check the progress of our rising fame.
Yet one, whilst imitation bears the sway,
Aspires to nobler heights, and points the way.
Be rous'd, my friends! his bold example view;
Let your own Bards be proud to copy you!
Should rigid critics reprobate our play,
At least the patriotic heart will say,
"Glorious our fall, since in a noble cause.
"The bold attempt alone demands applause."
Still may the wisdom of the Comic Muse
Exalt your merits, or your faults accuse.
But think not, tis her aim to be severe;--
We all are mortals, and as mortals err.
If candour pleases, we are truly blest;
Vice trembles, when compell'd to stand confess'd.
Let not light Censure on your faults offend,
Which aims not to expose them, but amend.
Thus does our Author to your candour trust;
Conscious, the free are generous, as just.

Characters

New-York   Maryland

	New-York	Maryland
Col. MANLY,	Mr Henry.	Mr Hallam.
DIMPLE,	Mr Hallam.	Mr Harper.
VANROUGH,	Mr Morris.	Mr Morris.
JESSAMY,	Mr Harper.	Mr Biddle.
JONATHAN,	Mr Wignell.	Mr Wignell.
CHARLOTTE,	Mrs Morris.	Mrs Morris.
MARIA,	Mrs Harper.	Mrs Harper.
LETITIA,	Mrs Kenna.	Mrs Williamson.
JENNY,	Miss Tuke.	Miss W. Tuke.

SERVANTS

SCENE, NEW-YORK.

ACT I.

Scene, an Apartment at CHARLOTTE'S.

CHARLOTTE and LETITIA discovered.

LETITIA
AND so, Charlotte, you really think the pocket-hoop unbecoming.

CHARLOTTE
No, I don't say so. It may be very becoming to saunter round the house of a rainy day; to visit my grand-mamma, or to go to Quakers' meeting: but to swim in a minuet, with the eyes of fifty well-dressed beaux upon me, to trip it in the Mall, or walk on the battery, give me the luxurious, jaunty, flowing, bell-hoop. It would have delighted you to have seen me the last evening, my charming girl! I was dangling o'er the battery with Billy Dimple; a knot of young fellows were upon the platform; as I passed them I faultered with one of the most bewitching false steps you ever saw, and then recovered myself with such a pretty confusion, flirting my hoop to discover a jet black shoe and brilliant buckle. Gad! how my little heart thrilled to hear the confused raptures of--"Demme, Jack, what a delicate foot!" "Ha! General, what a well-turned--"

LETITIA
Fie! fie! Charlotte [stopping her mouth], I protest you are quite a

libertine.

CHARLOTTE
Why, my dear little prude, are we not all such libertines? Do you think, when I sat tortured two hours under the hands of my friseur, and an hour more at my toilet, that I had any thoughts of my aunt Susan, or my cousin Betsey? though they are both allowed to be critical judges of dress.

LETITIA
Why, who should we dress to please, but those are judges of its merit?

CHARLOTTE
Why, a creature who does not know Buffon from Souflee--Man!--my Letitia--Man! for whom we dress, walk, dance, talk, lisp, languish, and smile. Does not the grave Spectator assure us that even our much bepraised diffidence, modesty, and blushes are all directed to make ourselves good wives and mothers as fast as we can? Why, I'll undertake with one flirt of this hoop to bring more beaux to my feet in one week than the grave Maria, and her sentimental circle, can do, by sighing sentiment till their hairs are grey.

LETITIA
Well, I won't argue with you; you always out-talk me; let us change the subject. I hear that Mr. Dimple and Maria are soon to be married.

CHARLOTTE
You hear true. I was consulted in the choice of the wedding clothes. She is to be married in a delicate white sattin, and has a monstrous

pretty brocaded lutestring for the second day. It would have done you good to have seen with what an affected indifference the dear sentimentalist turned over a thousand pretty things, just as if her heart did not palpitate with her approaching happiness, and at last made her choice and arranged her dress with such apathy as if she did not know that plain white sattin and a simple blond lace would shew her clear skin and dark hair to the greatest advantage.

LETITIA
But they say her indifference to dress, and even to the gentleman himself, is not entirely affected.

CHARLOTTE
How?

LETITIA
It is whispered that if Maria gives her hand to Mr. Dimple, it will be without her heart.

CHARLOTTE
Though the giving the heart is one of the last of all laughable considerations in the marriage of a girl of spirit, yet I should like to hear what antiquated notions the dear little piece of old-fashioned prudery has got in her head.

LETITIA
Why, you know that old Mr.
John-Richard-Robert-Jacob-Isaac-Abraham-Cornelius Van Dumpling, Billy

Dimple's father (for he has thought fit to soften his name, as well as manners, during his English tour), was the most intimate friend of Maria's father. The old folks, about a year before Mr. Van Dumpling's death, proposed this match: the young folks were accordingly introduced, and told they must love one another. Billy was then a good-natured, decent-dressing young fellow, with a little dash of the coxcomb, such as our young fellows of fortune usually have. At this time, I really believe she thought she loved him; and had they been married, I doubt not they might have jogged on, to the end of the chapter, a good kind of a sing-song lack-a-daysaical life, as other honest married folks do.

CHARLOTTE
Why did they not then marry?

LETITIA
Upon the death of his father, Billy went to England to see the world and rub off a little of the patroon rust. During his absence, Maria, like a good girl, to keep herself constant to her nown true-love, avoided company, and betook herself, for her amusement, to her books, and her dear Billy's letters. But, alas! how many ways has the mischievous demon of inconstancy of stealing into a woman's heart! Her love was destroyed by the very means she took to support it.

CHARLOTTE
How?--Oh! I have it--some likely young beau found the way to her study.

LETITIA
Be patient, Charlotte; your head so runs upon beaux. Why, she read Sir

Charles Grandison, Clarissa Harlow, Shenstone, and the Sentimental
Journey; and between whiles, as I said, Billy's letters. But, as her
taste improved, her love declined. The contrast was so striking
betwixt the good sense of her books and the flimsiness of her
love-letters, that she discovered she had unthinkingly engaged her hand
without her heart; and then the whole transaction, managed by the old
folks, now appeared so unsentimental, and looked so like bargaining for
a bale of goods, that she found she ought to have rejected, according
to every rule of romance, even the man of her choice, if imposed upon
her in that manner. Clary Harlow would have scorned such a match.

CHARLOTTE
Well, how was it on Mr. Dimple's return? Did he meet a more favourable
reception than his letters?

LETITIA
Much the same. She spoke of him with respect abroad, and with contempt
in her closet. She watched his conduct and conversation, and found
that he had by travelling, acquired the wickedness of Lovelace without
his wit, and the politeness of Sir Charles Grandison without his
generosity. The ruddy youth, who washed his face at the cistern every
morning, and swore and looked eternal love and constancy, was now
metamorphosed into a flippant, palid, polite beau, who devotes the
morning to his toilet, reads a few pages of Chesterfield's letters, and
then minces out, to put the infamous principles in practice upon every
woman he meets.

CHARLOTTE
But, if she is so apt at conjuring up these sentimental bugbears, why
does she not discard him at once?

LETITIA

Why, she thinks her word too sacred to be trifled with. Besides, her father, who has a great respect for the memory of his deceased friend, is ever telling her how he shall renew his years in their union, and repeating the dying injunctions of old Van Dumpling.

CHARLOTTE

A mighty pretty story! And so you would make me believe that the sensible Maria would give up Dumpling manor, and the all-accomplished Dimple as a husband, for the absurd, ridiculous reason, forsooth, because she despises and abhors him. Just as if a lady could not be privileged to spend a man's fortune, ride in his carriage, be called after his name, and call him her nown dear lovee when she wants money, without loving and respecting the great he-creature. Oh! my dear girl, you are a monstrous prude.

LETITIA

I don't say what I would do; I only intimate how I suppose she wishes to act.

CHARLOTTE

No, no, no! A fig for sentiment. If she breaks, or wishes to break, with Mr. Dimple, depend upon it, she has some other man in her eye. A woman rarely discards one lover until she is sure of another. Letitia little thinks what a clue I have to Dimple's conduct. The generous man submits to render himself disgusting to Maria, in order that she may leave him at liberty to address me. I must change the subject. [Aside, and rings a bell.

Enter SERVANT.

Frank, order the horses to.--Talking of marriage, did you hear that Sally Bloomsbury is going to be married next week to Mr. Indigo, the rich Carolinian?

LETITIA
Sally Bloomsbury married!--why, she is not yet in her teens.

CHARLOTTE
I do not know how that is, but you may depend upon it, 'tis a done affair. I have it from the best authority. There is my aunt Wyerly's Hannah. You know Hannah; though a black, she is a wench that was never caught in a lie in her life. Now, Hannah has a brother who courts Sarah, Mrs. Catgut the milliner's girl, and she told Hannah's brother, and Hannah, who, as I said before, is a girl of undoubted veracity, told it directly to me, that Mrs. Catgut was making a new cap for Miss Bloomsbury, which, as it was very dressy, it is very probable is designed for a wedding cap. Now, as she is to be married, who can it be to but to Mr. Indigo? Why, there is no other gentleman that visits at her papa's.

LETITIA
Say not a word more, Charlotte. Your intelligence is so direct and well grounded, it is almost a pity that it is not a piece of scandal.

CHARLOTTE
Oh! I am the pink of prudence. Though I cannot charge myself with ever having discredited a tea-party by my silence, yet I take care never to report any thing of my acquaintance, especially if it is to

their credit,--discredit, I mean,--until I have searched to the bottom
of it. It is true, there is infinite pleasure in this charitable
pursuit. Oh! how delicious to go and condole with the friends of some
backsliding sister, or to retire with some old dowager or maiden aunt
of the family, who love scandal so well that they cannot forbear
gratifying their appetite at the expense of the reputation of their
nearest relations! And then to return full fraught with a rich
collection of circumstances, to retail to the next circle of our
acquaintance under the strongest injunctions of secrecy,--ha, ha,
ha!--interlarding the melancholy tale with so many doleful shakes of
the head, and more doleful "Ah! who would have thought it! so amiable,
so prudent a young lady, as we all thought her, what a monstrous pity!
well, I have nothing to charge myself with; I acted the part of a
friend, I warned her of the principles of that rake, I told her what
would be the consequence; I told her so, I told her so."--Ha, ha, ha!

LETITIA
Ha, ha, ha! Well, but, Charlotte, you don't tell me what you think of
Miss Bloomsbury's match.

CHARLOTTE
Think! why I think it is probable she cried for a plaything, and they
have given her a husband. Well, well, well, the puling chit shall not
be deprived of her plaything: 'tis only exchanging London dolls for
American babies.--Apropos, of babies, have you heard what Mrs.
Affable's high-flying notions of delicacy have come to?

LETITIA
Who, she that was Miss Lovely?

CHARLOTTE
The same; she married Bob Affable of Schenectady. Don't you remember?

Enter SERVANT.

SERVANT.

Madam, the carriage is ready.

LETITIA
Shall we go to the stores first, or visiting?

CHARLOTTE
I should think it rather too early to visit, especially Mrs. Prim; you know she is so particular.

LETITIA
Well, but what of Mrs. Affable?

CHARLOTTE
Oh, I'll tell you as we go; come, come, let us hasten. I hear Mrs. Catgut has some of the prettiest caps arrived you ever saw. I shall die if I have not the first sight of them.   [Exeunt.

SCENE II.

A Room in VAN ROUGH'S House

MARIA sitting disconsolate at a Table, with Books, &c.

SONG.

I.

The sun sets in night, and the stars shun the day;
But glory remains when their lights fade away!
Begin, ye tormentors! your threats are in vain,
For the son of Alknomook shall never complain.

II.

Remember the arrows he shot from his bow;
Remember your chiefs by his hatchet laid low:
Why so slow?--do you wait till I shrink from the pain?
No--the son of Alknomook will never complain.

III.

Remember the wood where in ambush we lay,
And the scalps which we bore from your nation away:

Now the flame rises fast, you exult in my pain;
But the son of Alknomook can never complain.

IV.

I go to the land where my father is gone;
His ghost shall rejoice in the fame of his son:
Death comes like a friend, he relieves me from pain;
And thy son, Oh Alknomook! has scorn'd to complain.

There is something in this song which ever calls forth my affections.
The manly virtue of courage, that fortitude which steels the heart
against the keenest misfortunes, which interweaves the laurel of glory
amidst the instruments of torture and death, displays something so
noble, so exalted, that in despite of the prejudices of education I
cannot but admire it, even in a savage. The prepossession which our
sex is supposed to entertain for the character of a soldier is, I know,
a standing piece of raillery among the wits. A cockade, a lapell'd
coat, and a feather, they will tell you, are irresistible by a female
heart. Let it be so. Who is it that considers the helpless situation
of our sex, that does not see that we each moment stand in need of a
protector, and that a brave one too? Formed of the more delicate
materials of nature, endowed only with the softer passions, incapable,
from our ignorance of the world, to guard against the wiles of mankind,
our security for happiness often depends upon their generosity and
courage. Alas! how little of the former do we find! How
inconsistent! that man should be leagued to destroy that honour upon
which solely rests his respect and esteem. Ten thousand temptations
allure us, ten thousand passions betray us; yet the smallest deviation
from the path of rectitude is followed by the contempt and insult of
man, and the more remorseless pity of woman; years of penitence and

tears cannot wash away the stain, nor a life of virtue obliterate its remembrance. Reputation is the life of woman; yet courage to protect it is masculine and disgusting; and the only safe asylum a woman of delicacy can find is in the arms of a man of honour. How naturally, then, should we love the brave and the generous; how gratefully should we bless the arm raised for our protection, when nerv'd by virtue and directed by honour! Heaven grant that the man with whom I may be connected--may be connected! Whither has my imagination transported me--whither does it now lead me? Am I not indissolubly engaged, "by every obligation of honour which my own consent and my father's approbation can give," to a man who can never share my affections, and whom a few days hence it will be criminal for me to disapprove--to disapprove! would to heaven that were all--to despise. For, can the most frivolous manners, actuated by the most depraved heart, meet, or merit, anything but contempt from every woman of delicacy and sentiment?

[VAN ROUGH without. Mary!]

Ha! my father's voice--Sir!--

[Enter VAN ROUGH.

VAN ROUGH
What, Mary, always singing doleful ditties, and moping over these plaguy books.

MARIA
I hope, Sir, that it is not criminal to improve my mind with books, or to divert my melancholy with singing, at my leisure hours.

VAN ROUGH

Why, I don't know that, child; I don't know that. They us'd to say, when I was a young man, that if a woman knew how to make a pudding, and to keep herself out of fire and water, she knew enough for a wife. Now, what good have these books done you? have they not made you melancholy? as you call it. Pray, what right has a girl of your age to be in the dumps? haven't you everything your heart can wish; an't you going to be married to a young man of great fortune; an't you going to have the quit-rent of twenty miles square?

MARIA

One-hundredth part of the land, and a lease for life of the heart of a man I could love, would satisfy me.

VAN ROUGH

Pho, pho, pho! child; nonsense, downright nonsense, child. This comes of your reading your storybooks; your Charles Grandisons, your Sentimental Journals, and your Robinson Crusoes, and such other trumpery. No, no, no! child; it is money makes the mare go; keep your eye upon the main chance, Mary.

MARIA

Marriage, Sir, is, indeed, a very serious affair.

VAN ROUGH

You are right, child; you are right. I am sure I found it so, to my cost.

MARIA

I mean, Sir, that as marriage is a portion for life, and so intimately
involves our happiness, we cannot be too considerate in the choice of
our companion.

VAN ROUGH

Right, child; very right. A young woman should be very sober when she
is making her choice, but when she has once made it, as you have done,
I don't see why she should not be as merry as a grig; I am sure she has
reason enough to be so. Solomon says that "there is a time to laugh,
and a time to weep." Now, a time for a young woman to laugh is when she
has made sure of a good rich husband. Now, a time to cry, according to
you, Mary, is when she is making choice of him; but I should think that
a young woman's time to cry was when she despaired of getting one.
Why, there was your mother, now: to be sure, when I popp'd the question
to her she did look a little silly; but when she had once looked down
on her apron-strings, as all modest young women us'd to do, and drawled
out ye-s, she was as brisk and as merry as a bee.

MARIA

My honoured mother, Sir, had no motive to melancholy; she married the
man of her choice.

VAN ROUGH

The man of her choice! And pray, Mary, an't you going to marry the man
of your choice--what trumpery notion is this? It is these vile books
[throwing them away]. I'd have you to know, Mary, if you won't make
young Van Dumpling the man of your choice, you shall marry him as the
man of my choice.

MARIA
You terrify me, Sir. Indeed, Sir, I am all submission. My will is
yours.

VAN ROUGH
Why, that is the way your mother us'd to talk. "My will is yours, my
dear Mr. Van Rough, my will is yours"; but she took special care to
have her own way, though, for all that.

MARIA
Do not reflect upon my mother's memory, Sir--

VAN ROUGH
Why not, Mary, why not? She kept me from speaking my mind all her
life, and do you think she shall henpeck me now she is dead too? Come,
come; don't go to sniveling; be a good girl, and mind the main chance.
I'll see you well settled in the world.

MARIA
I do not doubt your love, Sir, and it is my duty to obey you. I will
endeavour to make my duty and inclination go hand in hand.

VAN ROUGH
Well, Well, Mary; do you be a good girl, mind the main chance, and
never mind inclination. Why, do you know that I have been down in the
cellar this very morning to examine a pipe of Madeira which I purchased
the week you were born, and mean to tap on your wedding day?--That pipe
cost me fifty pounds sterling. It was well worth sixty pounds; but I

over-reach'd Ben Bulkhead, the supercargo. I'll tell you the whole
story. You must know that--

Enter SERVANT.

SERVANT.

Sir, Mr. Transfer, the broker is below.   [Exit.

VAN ROUGH
Well, Mary, I must go. Remember, and be a good girl, and mind the main
chance.   [Exit.

MARIA, alone.

How deplorable is my situation! How distressing for a daughter to find
her heart militating with her filial duty! I know my father loves me
tenderly; why then do I reluctantly obey him? Heaven knows! with what
reluctance I should oppose the will of a parent, or set an example of
filial disobedience; at a parent's command, I could wed awkwardness and
deformity. Were the heart of my husband good, I would so magnify his
good qualities with the eye of conjugal affection, that the defects of
his person and manners should be lost in the emanation of his virtues.
At a father's command, I could embrace poverty. Were the poor man my
husband, I would learn resignation to my lot; I would enliven our
frugal meal with good humour, and chase away misfortune from our
cottage with a smile. At a father's command, I could almost submit to
what every female heart knows to be the most mortifying, to marry a
weak man, and blush at my husband's folly in every company I visited.
But to marry a depraved wretch, whose only virtue is a polished
exterior; who is actuated by the unmanly ambition of conquering the

defenceless; whose heart, insensible to the emotions of patriotism, dilates at the plaudits of every unthinking girl; whose laurels are the sighs and tears of the miserable victims of his specious behaviour,--can he, who has no regard for the peace and happiness of other families, ever have a due regard for the peace and happiness of his own? Would to heaven that my father were not so hasty in his temper? Surely, if I were to state my reasons for declining this match, he would not compel me to marry a man, whom, though my lips may solemnly promise to honour, I find my heart must ever despise.
[Exit.

END OF THE FIRST ACT.

ACT II.

SCENE I.

Enter CHARLOTTE and LETITIA.

CHARLOTTE [at entering].

BETTY, take those things out of the carriage and carry them to my chamber; see that you don't tumble them. My dear, I protest, I think it was the homeliest of the whole. I declare I was almost tempted to return and change it.

LETITIA
Why would you take it?

CHARLOTTE
Didn't Mrs. Catgut say it was the most fashionable?

LETITIA
But, my dear, it will never fit becomingly on you.

CHARLOTTE
I know that; but did you not hear Mrs. Catgut say it was fashionable?

LETITIA
Did you see that sweet airy cap with the white sprig?

CHARLOTTE
Yes, and I longed to take it; but, my dear, what could I do? Did not
Mrs. Catgut say it was the most fashionable; and if I had not taken it,
was not that awkward, gawky, Sally Slender, ready to purchase it
immediately?

LETITIA
Did you observe how she tumbled over the things at the next shop, and
then went off without purchasing anything, nor even thanking the poor
man for his trouble? But, of all the awkward creatures, did you see
Miss Blouze endeavouring to thrust her unmerciful arm into those small
kid gloves?

CHARLOTTE
Ha, ha, ha, ha!

LETITIA
Then did you take notice with what an affected warmth of friendship she
and Miss Wasp met? when all their acquaintance know how much pleasure
they take in abusing each other in every company.

CHARLOTTE
Lud! Letitia, is that so extraordinary? Why, my dear, I hope you are
not going to turn sentimentalist. Scandal, you know, is but amusing
ourselves with the faults, foibles, follies, and reputations of our
friends; indeed, I don't know why we should have friends, if we are not
at liberty to make use of them. But no person is so ignorant of the
world as to suppose, because I amuse myself with a lady's faults, that
I am obliged to quarrel with her person every time we meet: believe me,
my dear, we should have very few acquaintance at that rate.

SERVANT enters and delivers a letter to CHARLOTTE, and--[Exit.

CHARLOTTE
You'll excuse me, my dear.

[Opens and reads to herself.

LETITIA
Oh, quite excusable.

CHARLOTTE
As I hope to be married, my brother Henry is in the city.

LETITIA
What, your brother, Colonel Manly?

CHARLOTTE
Yes, my dear; the only brother I have in the world.

LETITIA
Was he never in this city?

CHARLOTTE
Never nearer than Harlem Heights, where he lay with his regiment.

LETITIA
What sort of a being is this brother of yours? If he is as chatty, as
pretty, as sprightly as you, half the belles in the city will be
pulling caps for him.

CHARLOTTE
My brother is the very counterpart and reverse of me: I am gay, he is
grave; I am airy, he is solid; I am ever selecting the most pleasing
objects for my laughter, he has a tear for every pitiful one. And
thus, whilst he is plucking the briars and thorns from the path of the
unfortunate, I am strewing my own path with roses.

LETITIA
My sweet friend, not quite so poetical, and a little more particular.

CHARLOTTE
Hands off, Letitia. I feel the rage of simile upon me; I can't talk to
you in any other way. My brother has a heart replete with the noblest
sentiments, but then, it is like--it is like--Oh! you provoking girl,
you have deranged all my ideas--it is like--Oh! I have it--his heart is
like an old maiden lady's bandbox; it contains many costly things,
arranged with the most scrupulous nicety, yet the misfortune is that

they are too delicate, costly, and antiquated for common use.

LETITIA
By what I can pick out of your flowery description, your brother is no beau.

CHARLOTTE
No, indeed; he makes no pretension to the character. He'd ride, or rather fly, an hundred miles to relieve a distressed object, or to do a gallant act in the service of his country; but should you drop your fan or bouquet in his presence, it is ten to one that some beau at the farther end of the room would have the honour of presenting it to you before he had observed that it fell. I'll tell you one of his antiquated, anti-gallant notions. He said once in my presence, in a room full of company,--would you believe it?--in a large circle of ladies, that the best evidence a gentleman could give a young lady of his respect and affection was to endeavour in a friendly manner to rectify her foibles. I protest I was crimson to the eyes, upon reflecting that I was known as his sister.

LETITIA
Insupportable creature! tell a lady of her faults! if he is so grave, I fear I have no chance of captivating him.

CHARLOTTE
His conversation is like a rich, old-fashioned brocade,--it will stand alone; every sentence is a sentiment. Now you may judge what a time I had with him, in my twelve months' visit to my father. He read me such lectures, out of pure brotherly affection, against the extremes of

fashion, dress, flirting, and coquetry, and all the other dear things
which he knows I doat upon, that I protest his conversation made me as
melancholy as if I had been at church; and heaven knows, though I never
prayed to go there but on one occasion, yet I would have exchanged his
conversation for a psalm and a sermon. Church is rather melancholy, to
be sure; but then I can ogle the beaux, and be regaled with "here
endeth the first lesson," but his brotherly here, you would think had
no end. You captivate him! Why, my dear, he would as soon fall in
love with a box of Italian flowers. There is Maria, now, if she were
not engaged, she might do something. Oh! how I should like to see that
pair of pensorosos together, looking as grave as two sailors' wives of
a stormy night, with a flow of sentiment meandering through their
conversation like purling streams in modern poetry.

LETITIA
Oh! my dear fanciful--

CHARLOTTE
Hush! I hear some person coming through the entry.

Enter SERVANT.

SERVANT.

Madam, there's a gentleman below who calls himself Colonel Manly; do
you chuse to be at home?

CHARLOTTE
Shew him in. [Exit Servant.] Now for a sober face.

Enter Colonel MANLY.

MANLY

My dear Charlotte, I am happy that I once more enfold you within the arms of fraternal affection. I know you are going to ask (amiable impatience!) how our parents do,--the venerable pair transmit you their blessing by me. They totter on the verge of a well-spent life, and wish only to see their children settled in the world, to depart in peace.

CHARLOTTE

I am very happy to hear that they are well. [Coolly.] Brother, will you give me leave to introduce you to our uncle's ward, one of my most intimate friends?

MANLY [saluting Letitia].

I ought to regard your friends as my own.

CHARLOTTE

Come, Letitia, do give us a little dash of your vivacity; my brother is so sentimental and so grave, that I protest he'll give us the vapours.

MANLY

Though sentiment and gravity, I know, are banished the polite world, yet I hoped they might find some countenance in the meeting of such near connections as brother and sister.

CHARLOTTE
Positively, brother, if you go one step further in this strain, you
will set me crying, and that, you know, would spoil my eyes; and then I
should never get the husband which our good papa and mamma have so
kindly wished me--never be established in the world.

MANLY
Forgive me, my sister,--I am no enemy to mirth; I love your
sprightliness; and I hope it will one day enliven the hours of some
worthy man; but when I mention the respectable authors of my
existence,--the cherishers and protectors of my helpless infancy, whose
hearts glow with such fondness and attachment that they would willingly
lay down their lives for my welfare,--you will excuse me if I am so
unfashionable as to speak of them with some degree of respect and
reverence.

CHARLOTTE
Well, well, brother; if you won't be gay, we'll not differ; I will be
as grave as you wish. [Affects gravity.] And so, brother, you have
come to the city to exchange some of your commutation notes for a
little pleasure?

MANLY
Indeed you are mistaken; my errand is not of amusement, but business;
and as I neither drink nor game, my expenses will be so trivial, I
shall have no occasion to sell my notes.

CHARLOTTE
Then you won't have occasion to do a very good thing. Why, here was

the Vermont General--he came down some time since, sold all his musty
notes at one stroke, and then laid the cash out in trinkets for his
dear Fanny. I want a dozen pretty things myself; have you got the
notes with you?

MANLY
I shall be ever willing to contribute, as far as it is in my power, to
adorn or in any way to please my sister; yet I hope I shall never be
obliged for this to sell my notes. I may be romantic, but I preserve
them as a sacred deposit. Their full amount is justly due to me, but
as embarrassments, the natural consequences of a long war, disable my
country from supporting its credit, I shall wait with patience until it
is rich enough to discharge them. If that is not in my day, they shall
be transmitted as an honourable certificate to posterity, that I have
humbly imitated our illustrious WASHINGTON, in having exposed my
health
and life in the service of my country, without reaping any other reward
than the glory of conquering in so arduous a contest.

CHARLOTTE
Well said heroics. Why, my dear Henry, you have such a lofty way of
saying things, that I protest I almost tremble at the thought of
introducing you to the polite circles in the city. The belles would
think you were a player run mad, with your head filled with old scraps
of tragedy; and as to the beaux, they might admire, because they would
not understand you. But, however, I must, I believe, introduce you to
two or three ladies of my acquaintance.

LETITIA
And that will make him acquainted with thirty or forty beaux.

CHARLOTTE
Oh! brother, you don't know what a fund of happiness you have in store.

MANLY
I fear, sister, I have not refinement sufficient to enjoy it.

CHARLOTTE
Oh! you cannot fail being pleased.

LETITIA
Our ladies are so delicate and dressy.

CHARLOTTE
And our beaux so dressy and delicate.

LETITIA
Our ladies chat and flirt so agreeably.

CHARLOTTE
And our beaux simper and bow so gracefully.

LETITIA
With their hair so trim and neat.

CHARLOTTE
And their faces so soft and sleek.

LETITIA
Their buckles so tonish and bright.

CHARLOTTE
And their hands so slender and white.

LETITIA
I vow, Charlotte, we are quite poetical.

CHARLOTTE
And then, brother, the faces of the beaux are of such a lily-white hue!
None of that horrid robustness of constitution, that vulgar corn-fed
glow of health, which can only serve to alarm an unmarried lady with
apprehension, and prove a melancholy memento to a married one, that she
can never hope for the happiness of being a widow. I will say this to
the credit of our city beaux, that such is the delicacy of their
complexion, dress, and address, that, even had I no reliance upon the
honour of the dear Adonises, I would trust myself in any possible
situation with them, without the least apprehensions of rudeness.

MANLY
Sister Charlotte!

CHARLOTTE

Now, now, now, brother [interrupting him], now don't go to spoil my mirth with a dash of your gravity; I am so glad to see you, I am in tiptop spirits. Oh! that you could be with us at a little snug party. There is Billy Simper, Jack Chaffe, and Colonel Van Titter, Miss Promonade, and the two Miss Tambours, sometimes make a party, with some other ladies, in a side-box at the play. Everything is conducted with such decorum. First we bow round to the company in general, then to each one in particular, then we have so many inquiries after each other's health, and we are so happy to meet each other, and it is so many ages since we last had that pleasure, and if a married lady is in company, we have such a sweet dissertation upon her son Bobby's chin-cough; then the curtain rises, then our sensibility is all awake, and then, by the mere force of apprehension, we torture some harmless expression into a double meaning, which the poor author never dreamt of, and then we have recourse to our fans, and then we blush, and then the gentlemen jog one another, peep under the fan, and make the prettiest remarks; and then we giggle and they simper, and they giggle and we simper, and then the curtain drops, and then for nuts and oranges, and then we bow, and it's pray, Ma'am, take it, and pray, Sir, keep it, and oh! not for the world, Sir; and then the curtain rises again, and then we blush and giggle and simper and bow all over again. Oh! the sentimental charms of a side-box conversation! [All laugh.]

MANLY

Well, sister, I join heartily with you in the laugh; for, in my opinion, it is as justifiable to laugh at folly as it is reprehensible to ridicule misfortune.

CHARLOTTE

Well, but, brother, positively I can't introduce you in these clothes:

why, your coat looks as if it were calculated for the vulgar purpose of keeping yourself comfortable.

MANLY
This coat was my regimental coat in the late war. The public tumults of our state have induced me to buckle on the sword in support of that government which I once fought to establish. I can only say, sister, that there was a time when this coat was respectable, and some people even thought that those men who had endured so many winter campaigns in the service of their country, without bread, clothing, or pay, at least deserved that the poverty of their appearance should not be ridiculed.

CHARLOTTE
We agree in opinion entirely, brother, though it would not have done for me to have said it: it is the coat makes the man respectable. In the time of the war, when we were almost frightened to death, why, your coat was respectable, that is, fashionable; now another kind of coat is fashionable, that is, respectable. And pray direct the taylor to make yours the height of the fashion.

MANLY
Though it is of little consequence to me of what shape my coat is, yet, as to the height of the fashion, there you will please to excuse me, sister. You know my sentiments on that subject. I have often lamented the advantage which the French have over us in that particular. In Paris, the fashions have their dawnings, their routine, and declensions, and depend as much upon the caprice of the day as in other countries; but there every lady assumes a right to deviate from the general ton as far as will be of advantage to her own appearance. In America, the cry is, what is the fashion? and we follow it

indiscriminately, because it is so.

CHARLOTTE Therefore it is, that when large hoops are in fashion, we often see many a plump girl lost in the immensity of a hoop-petticoat, whose want of height and en-bon-point would never have been remarked in any other dress. When the high head-dress is the mode, how then do we see a lofty cushion, with a profusion of gauze, feathers, and ribband, supported by a face no bigger than an apple! whilst a broad full-faced lady, who really would have appeared tolerably handsome in a large head-dress, looks with her smart chapeau as masculine as a soldier.

MANLY
But remember, my dear sister, and I wish all my fair country-women would recollect, that the only excuse a young lady can have for going extravagantly into a fashion is because it makes her look extravagantly handsome.--Ladies, I must wish you a good morning.

CHARLOTTE
But, brother, you are going to make home with us.

MANLY
Indeed I cannot. I have seen my uncle and explained that matter.

CHARLOTTE
Come and dine with us, then. We have a family dinner about half-past four o'clock.

MANLY
I am engaged to dine with the Spanish ambassador. I was introduced to

him by an old brother officer; and instead of freezing me with a cold card of compliment to dine with him ten days hence, he, with the true old Castilian frankness, in a friendly manner, asked me to dine with him to-day--an honour I could not refuse. Sister, adieu--Madam, your most obedient--[Exit.

CHARLOTTE
I will wait upon you to the door, brother; I have something particular to say to you.   [Exit.

LETITIA, alone.

What a pair!--She the pink of flirtation, he the essence of everything that is outre and gloomy.--I think I have completely deceived Charlotte by my manner of speaking of Mr. Dimple; she's too much the friend of Maria to be confided in. He is certainly rendering himself disagreeable to Maria, in order to break with her and proffer his hand to me. This is what the delicate fellow hinted in our last conversation. [Exit.

SCENE II. The Mall.

Enter JESSAMY.

Positively this Mall is a very pretty place. I hope the cits won't
ruin it by repairs. To be sure, it won't do to speak of in the same
day with Ranelagh or Vauxhall; however, it's a fine place for a young
fellow to display his person to advantage. Indeed, nothing is lost
here; the girls have taste, and I am very happy to find they have
adopted the elegant London fashion of looking back, after a genteel
fellow like me has passed them.--Ah! who comes here? This, by his
awkwardness, must be the Yankee colonel's servant. I'll accost him.

Enter JONATHAN.

JESSAMY
Votre tres-humble serviteur, Monsieur. I understand Colonel Manly, the
Yankee officer, has the honour of your services.

JONATHAN
Sir!--

JESSAMY
I say, Sir, I understand that Colonel Manly has the honour of having
you for a servant.

JONATHAN

Servant! Sir, do you take me for a neger,--I am Colonel Manly's waiter.

JESSAMY

A true Yankee distinction, egad, without a difference. Why, Sir, do you not perform all the offices of a servant? do you not even blacken his boots?

JONATHAN

Yes; I do grease them a bit sometimes; but I am a true blue son of liberty, for all that. Father said I should come as Colonel Manly's waiter, to see the world, and all that; but no man shall master me. My father has as good a farm as the colonel.

JESSAMY

Well, Sir, we will not quarrel about terms upon the eve of an acquaintance from which I promise myself so much satisfaction;--therefore, sans ceremonie--

JONATHAN

What?--

JESSAMY

I say I am extremely happy to see Colonel Manly's waiter.

JONATHAN

Well, and I vow, too, I am pretty considerably glad to see you; but

what the dogs need of all this outlandish lingo? Who may you be, Sir,
if I may be so bold?

JESSAMY
I have the honour to be Mr. Dimple's servant, or, if you please,
waiter. We lodge under the same roof, and should be glad of the honour
of your acquaintance.

JONATHAN
You a waiter! by the living jingo, you look so topping, I took you for
one of the agents to Congress.

JESSAMY
The brute has discernment, notwithstanding his appearance.--Give me
leave to say I wonder then at your familiarity.

JONATHAN
Why, as to the matter of that, Mr.--; pray, what's your name?

JESSAMY
Jessamy, at your service.

JONATHAN
Why, I swear we don't make any great matter of distinction in our state
between quality and other folks.

JESSAMY

This is, indeed, a levelling principle.--I hope, Mr. Jonathan, you have
not taken part with the insurgents.

JONATHAN

Why, since General Shays has sneaked off and given us the bag to hold,
I don't care to give my opinion; but you'll promise not to tell--put
your ear this way--you won't tell?--I vow I did think the sturgeons
were right.

JESSAMY

I thought, Mr. Jonathan, you Massachusetts men always argued with a gun
in your hand. Why didn't you join them?

JONATHAN

Why, the colonel is one of those folks called the Shin--Shin--dang it
all, I can't speak them lignum vitae words--you know who I mean--there
is a company of them--they wear a china goose at their button-hole--a
kind of gilt thing.--Now the colonel told father and brother,--you must
know there are, let me see--there is Elnathan, Silas, and Barnabas,
Tabitha--no, no, she's a she--tarnation, now I have it--there's
Elnathan, Silas, Barnabas, Jonathan, that's I--seven of us, six went
into the wars, and I staid at home to take care of mother. Colonel
said that it was a burning shame for the true blue Bunker Hill sons of
liberty, who had fought Governor Hutchinson, Lord North, and the Devil,
to have any hand in kicking up a cursed dust against a government which
we had, every mother's son of us, a hand in making.

JESSAMY

Bravo!--Well, have you been abroad in the city since your arrival?

What have you seen that is curious and entertaining?

JONATHAN

Oh! I have seen a power of fine sights. I went to see two marble-stone men and a leaden horse that stands out in doors in all weathers; and when I came where they was, one had got no head, and t'other wern't there. They said as how the leaden man was a damn'd tory, and that he took wit in his anger and rode off in the time of the troubles.

JESSAMY

But this was not the end of your excursion?

JONATHAN

Oh, no; I went to a place they call Holy Ground. Now I counted this was a place where folks go to meeting; so I put my hymn-book in my pocket, and walked softly and grave as a minister; and when I came there, the dogs a bit of a meeting-house could I see. At last I spied a young gentlewoman standing by one of the seats which they have here at the doors. I took her to be the deacon's daughter, and she looked so kind, and so obliging, that I thought I would go and ask her the way to lecture, and--would you think it?--she called me dear, and sweeting, and honey, just as if we were married: by the living jingo, I had a month's mind to buss her.

JESSAMY

Well, but how did it end?

JONATHAN
Why, as I was standing talking with her, a parcel of sailor men and boys got round me, the snarl-headed curs fell a-kicking and cursing of me at such a tarnal rate, that I vow I was glad to take to my heels and split home, right off, tail on end, like a stream of chalk.

JESSAMY
Why, my dear friend, you are not acquainted with the city; that girl you saw was a--[whispers.]

JONATHAN
Mercy on my soul! was that young woman a harlot!--Well! if this is New-York Holy Ground, what must the Holy-day Ground be!

JESSAMY
Well, you should not judge of the city too rashly. We have a number of elegant, fine girls here that make a man's leisure hours pass very agreeably. I would esteem it an honour to announce you to some of them.--Gad! that announce is a select word; I wonder where I picked it up.

JONATHAN
I don't want to know them.

JESSAMY
Come, come, my dear friend, I see that I must assume the honour of being the director of your amusements. Nature has given us passions, and youth and opportunity stimulate to gratify them. It is no shame, my dear Blueskin, for a man to amuse himself with a little gallantry.

JONATHAN

Girl huntry! I don't altogether understand. I never played at that game. I know how to play hunt the squirrel, but I can't play anything with the girls; I am as good as married.

JESSAMY

Vulgar, horrid brute! Married, and above a hundred miles from his wife, and thinks that an objection to his making love to every woman he meets! He never can have read, no, he never can have been in a room with a volume of the divine Chesterfield.--So you are married?

JONATHAN

No, I don't say so; I said I was as good as married, a kind of promise.

JESSAMY

As good as married!--

JONATHAN

Why, yes; there's Tabitha Wymen, the deacon's daughter, at home; she and I have been courting a great while, and folks say as how we are to be married; and so I broke a piece of money with her when we parted, and she promised not to spark it with Solomon Dyer while I am gone. You wouldn't have me false to my true-love, would you?

JESSAMY

May be you have another reason for constancy; possibly the young lady has a fortune? Ha! Mr. Jonathan, the solid charms: the chains of love are never so binding as when the links are made of gold.

JONATHAN
Why, as to fortune, I must needs say her father is pretty dumb rich; he went representative for our town last year. He will give her--let me see--four times seven is--seven times four--nought and carry one,-- he will give her twenty acres of land--somewhat rocky though--a Bible, and a cow.

JESSAMY
Twenty acres of rock, a Bible, and a cow! Why, my dear Mr. Jonathan, we have servant-maids, or, as you would more elegantly express it, waitresses, in this city, who collect more in one year from their mistresses' cast clothes.

JONATHAN
You don't say so!--

JESSAMY
Yes, and I'll introduce to one of them. There is a little lump of flesh and delicacy that lives at next door, waitress to Miss Maria; we often see her on the stoop.

JONATHAN
But are you sure she would be courted by me?

JESSAMY
Never doubt it; remember a faint heart never--blisters on my tongue--I was going to be guilty of a vile proverb; flat against the authority of Chesterfield. I say there can be no doubt that the brilliancy of your

merit will secure you a favourable reception.

JONATHAN
Well, but what must I say to her?

JESSAMY
Say to her! why, my dear friend, though I admire your profound
knowledge on every other subject, yet, you will pardon my saying that
your want of opportunity has made the female heart escape the poignancy
of your penetration. Say to her! Why, when a man goes a-courting, and
hopes for success, he must begin with doing, and not saying.

JONATHAN
Well, what must I do?

JESSAMY
Why, when you are introduced you must make five or six elegant bows.

JONATHAN
Six elegant bows! I understand that; six, you say? Well--

JESSAMY
Then you must press and kiss her hand; then press and kiss, and so on
to her lips and cheeks; then talk as much as you can about hearts,
darts, flames, nectar, and ambrosia--the more incoherent the better.

JONATHAN
Well, but suppose she should be angry with I?

JESSAMY
Why, if she should pretend--please to observe, Mr. Jonathan--if she
should pretend to be offended, you must-- But I'll tell you how my
master acted in such a case: He was seated by a young lady of eighteen
upon a sofa, plucking with a wanton hand the blooming sweets of youth
and beauty. When the lady thought it necessary to check his ardour,
she called up a frown upon her lovely face, so irresistibly alluring,
that it would have warmed the frozen bosom of age; remember, said she,
putting her delicate arm upon his, remember your character and my
honour. My master instantly dropped upon his knees, with eyes swimming
with love, cheeks glowing with desire, and in the gentlest modulation
of voice he said: My dear Caroline, in a few months our hands will be
indissolubly united at the altar; our hearts I feel are already so; the
favours you now grant as evidence of your affection are favours indeed;
yet, when the ceremony is once past, what will now be received with
rapture will then be attributed to duty.

JONATHAN
Well, and what was the consequence?

JESSAMY
The consequence!--Ah! forgive me, my dear friend, but you New England
gentlemen have such a laudable curiosity of seeing the bottom of
everything;--why, to be honest, I confess I saw the blooming cherub of
a consequence smiling in its angelic mother's arms, about ten months
afterwards.

JONATHAN
Well, if I follow all your plans, make them six bows, and all that,
shall I have such little cherubim consequences?

JESSAMY
Undoubtedly.--What are you musing upon?

JONATHAN
You say you'll certainly make me acquainted?-- Why, I was thinking
then how I should contrive to pass this broken piece of silver--won't
it buy a sugar-dram?

JESSAMY
What is that, the love-token from the deacon's daughter?--You come on
bravely. But I must hasten to my master. Adieu, my dear friend.

JONATHAN
Stay, Mr. Jessamy--must I buss her when I am introduced to her?

JESSAMY
I told you, you must kiss her.

JONATHAN
Well, but must I buss her?

JESSAMY
Why, kiss and buss, and buss and kiss, is all one.

JONATHAN
Oh! my dear friend, though you have a profound knowledge of all, a pungency of tribulation, you don't know everything.
[Exit.

JESSAMY, alone.

Well, certainly I improve; my master could not have insinuated himself with more address into the heart of a man he despised. Now will this blundering dog sicken Jenny with his nauseous pawings, until she flies into my arms for very ease. How sweet will the contrast be between the blundering Jonathan and the courtly and accomplished Jessamy!

END OF THE SECOND ACT.

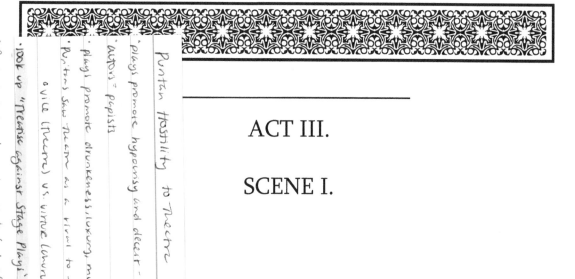

ACT III.

SCENE I.

at a Toilet, Reading.

neral but one object, which is their beauty." Very
ely very true. "Nature has hardly formed a woman
sensible to flattery upon her person." Extremely
ay's delightful experience confirms this. "If
g that she must, in some degree, be conscious of
she thinks, make ample amends for it." The
proof of this. Upon my telling the distasteful
r, that her countenance spoke the pensive language
t Lady Wortley Montague declared that if the
the garb of innocence, the face would be the
last part which would be admired, as Monsieur Milton expresses it; she
grinn'd horribly, a ghastly smile. "If her figure is deformed, she
thinks her face counterbalances it."

Enter JESSAMY with letters.

DIMPLE
Where got you these, Jessamy?

JESSAMY
Sir, the English packet is arrived.

DIMPLE opens and reads a letter enclosing notes.

"Sir,

"I have drawn bills on you in favour of Messrs. Van Cash and Co. as
per margin. I have taken up your note to Col. Piquet, and discharged
your debts to my Lord Lurcher and Sir Harry Rook. I herewith enclose
you copies of the bills, which I have no doubt will be immediately
honoured. On failure, I shall empower some lawyer in your country to
recover the amounts.

"I am, Sir,
  "Your most humble servant,
    "JOHN HAZARD."

Now, did not my lord expressly say that it was unbecoming a well-bred
man to be in a passion, I confess I should be ruffled. [Reads.]
"There is no accident so unfortunate, which a wise man may not turn to
his advantage; nor any accident so fortunate, which a fool will not
turn to his disadvantage." True, my lord; but how advantage can be
derived from this I can't see. Chesterfield himself, who made,
however, the worst practice of the most excellent precepts, was never
in so embarrassing a situation. I love the person of Charlotte, and it
is necessary I should command the fortune of Letitia. As to Maria!--I
doubt not by my sang-froid behaviour I shall compel her to decline the

match; but the blame must not fall upon me. A prudent man, as my lord says, should take all the credit of a good action to himself, and throw the discredit of a bad one upon others. I must break with Maria, marry Letitia, and as for Charlotte--why, Charlotte must be a companion to my wife.--Here, Jessamy!

Enter JESSAMY.

DIMPLE folds and seals two letters.

DIMPLE
Here, Jessamy, take this letter to my love.

[Gives one.

JESSAMY
To which of your honour's loves?--Oh! [reading] to Miss Letitia, your honour's rich love.

DIMPLE
And this [delivers another] to Miss Charlotte Manly. See that you deliver them privately.

JESSAMY
Yes, your honour.   [Going.

DIMPLE
Jessamy, who are these strange lodgers that came to the house last night?

JESSAMY

Why, the master is a Yankee colonel; I have not seen much of him; but the man is the most unpolished animal your honour ever disgraced your eyes by looking upon. I have had one of the most outre conversations with him!--He really has a most prodigious effect upon my risibility.

DIMPLE

I ought, according to every rule of Chesterfield, to wait on him and insinuate myself into his good graces.--Jessamy, wait on the colonel with my compliments, and if he is disengaged I will do myself the honour of paying him my respects.--Some ignorant, unpolished boor--

JESSAMY goes off and returns.

JESSAMY

Sir, the colonel is gone out, and Jonathan his servant says that he is gone to stretch his legs upon the Mall.--Stretch his legs! what an indelicacy of diction!

DIMPLE

Very well. Reach me my hat and sword. I'll accost him there, in my way to Letitia's, as by accident; pretend to be struck by his person and address, and endeavour to steal into his confidence. Jessamy, I have no business for you at present.   [Exit.

JESSAMY [taking up the book].

My master and I obtain our knowledge from the same source;--though, gad! I think myself much the prettier fellow of the two. [Surveying

himself in the glass.] That was a brilliant thought, to insinuate that
I folded my master's letters for him; the folding is so neat, that it
does honour to the operator. I once intended to have insinuated that I
wrote his letters too; but that was before I saw them; it won't do now;
no honour there, positively.--"Nothing looks more vulgar, [reading
affectedly] ordinary, and illiberal than ugly, uneven, and ragged
nails; the ends of which should be kept even and clean, not tipped with
black, and cut in small segments of circles."--Segments of circles!
surely my lord did not consider that he wrote for the beaux. Segments
of circles; what a crabbed term! Now I dare answer that my master,
with all his learning, does not know that this means, according to the
present mode, let the nails grow long, and then cut them off even at
top. [Laughing without.] Ha! that's Jenny's titter. I protest I
despair of ever teaching that girl to laugh; she has something so
execrably natural in her laugh, that I declare it absolutely
discomposes my nerves. How came she into our house! [Calls.] Jenny!

Enter JENNY.

JESSAMY
Prythee, Jenny, don't spoil your fine face with laughing.

JENNY
Why, mustn't I laugh, Mr. Jessamy?

JESSAMY
You may smile, but, as my lord says, nothing can authorise a laugh.

JENNY
Well, but I can't help laughing.--Have you seen him, Mr. Jessamy? ha, ha, ha!

JESSAMY
Seen whom?

JENNY
Why, Jonathan, the New England colonel's servant. Do you know he was at the play last night, and the stupid creature don't know where he has been. He would not go to a play for the world; he thinks it was a show, as he calls it.

JESSAMY
As ignorant and unpolished as he is, do you know, Miss Jenny, that I propose to introduce him to the honour of your acquaintance?

JENNY
Introduce him to me! for what?

JESSAMY
Why, my lovely girl, that you may take him under your protection, as Madame Ramboulliet did young Stanhope; that you may, by your plastic hand, mould this uncouth cub into a gentleman. He is to make love to you.

JENNY
Make love to me!--

JESSAMY

Yes, Mistress Jenny, make love to you; and, I doubt not, when he shall become domesticated in your kitchen, that this boor, under your auspices, will soon become un amiable petit Jonathan.

JENNY

I must say, Mr. Jessamy, if he copies after me, he will be vastly, monstrously polite.

JESSAMY

Stay here one moment, and I will call him.--Jonathan!--Mr. Jonathan!--[Calls.]

JONATHAN [within]

Holla! there.--[Enters.] You promise to stand by me--six bows you say. [Bows.]

JESSAMY

Mrs. Jenny, I have the honour of presenting Mr. Jonathan, Colonel Manly's waiter, to you. I am extremely happy that I have it in my power to make two worthy people acquainted with each other's merits.

JENNY

So, Mr. Jonathan, I hear you were at the play last night.

JONATHAN
At the play! why, did you think I went to the devil's drawing-room?

JENNY
The devil's drawing-room!

JONATHAN
Yes; why an't cards and dice the devil's device, and the play-house the
shop where the devil hangs out the vanities of the world upon the
tenter-hooks of temptation? I believe you have not heard how they were
acting the old boy one night, and the wicked one came among them sure
enough, and went right off in a storm, and carried one quarter of the
play-house with him. Oh! no, no, no! you won't catch me at a
play-house, I warrant you.

JENNY
Well, Mr. Jonathan, though I don't scruple your veracity, I have some
reasons for believing you were there: pray, where were you about six
o'clock?

JONATHAN
Why, I went to see one Mr. Morrison, the hocus pocus man; they said as
how he could eat a case knife.

JENNY
Well, and how did you find the place?

JONATHAN

As I was going about here and there, to and again, to find it, I saw a
great crowd of folks going into a long entry that had lantherns over
the door; so I asked a man whether that was not the place where they
played hocus pocus? He was a very civil, kind man, though he did speak
like the Hessians; he lifted up his eyes and said, "They play hocus
pocus tricks enough there, Got knows, mine friend."

JENNY

Well--

JONATHAN

So I went right in, and they shewed me away, clean up to the garret,
just like meeting-house gallery. And so I saw a bower of topping
folks, all sitting round in little cabbins, "just like father's
corn-cribs"; and then there was such a squeaking with the fiddles, and
such a tarnal blaze with the lights, my head was near turned. At last
the people that sat near me set up such a hissing--hiss--like so many
mad cats; and then they went thump, thump, thump, just like our Peleg
threshing wheat, and stampt away, just like the nation; and called out
for one Mr. Langolee,--I suppose he helps act the tricks.

JENNY

Well, and what did you do all this time?

JONATHAN

Gor, I--I liked the fun, and so I thumpt away, and hiss'd as lustily as
the best of 'em. One sailor-looking man that sat by me, seeing me
stamp, and knowing I was a cute fellow, because I could make a roaring

noise, clapt me on the shoulder and said, "You are a d---d hearty cock, smite my timbers!" I told him so I was, but I thought he need not swear so, and make use of such naughty words.

JESSAMY
The savage!--Well, and did you see the man with his tricks?

JONATHAN
Why, I vow, as I was looking out for him, they lifted up a great green cloth and let us look right into the next neighbor's house. Have you a good many houses in New-York made so in that 'ere way?

JENNY
Not many; but did you see the family?

JONATHAN
Yes, swamp it; I see'd the family.

JENNY
Well, and how did you like them?

JONATHAN
Why, I vow they were pretty much like other families;--there was a poor, good-natured, curse of a husband, and a sad rantipole of a wife.

JENNY
But did you see no other folks?

JONATHAN
Yes. There was one youngster; they called him Mr. Joseph; he talked as
sober and as pious as a minister; but, like some ministers that I know,
he was a sly tike in his heart for all that. He was going to ask a
young woman to spark it with him, and--the Lord have mercy on my
soul!--she was another man's wife.

JESSAMY
The Wabash!

JENNY
And did you see any more folks?

JONATHAN
Why, they came on as thick as mustard. For my part, I thought the
house was haunted. There was a soldier fellow, who talked about his
row de dow, dow, and courted a young woman; but, of all the cute folk I
saw, I liked one little fellow--

JENNY
Aye! who was he?

JONATHAN
Why, he had red hair, and a little round plump face like mine, only not

altogether so handsome. His name was--Darby;--that was his baptizing
name; his other name I forgot. Oh! it was Wig--Wag--Wag-all,
 Darby Wag-all,--pray, do you know him?--I should
like to take a sling with him, or a drap of cyder with a pepper-pod in
it, to make it warm and comfortable.

JENNY
I can't say I have that pleasure.

JONATHAN
I wish you did; he is a cute fellow. But there was one thing I didn't
like in that Mr. Darby; and that was, he was afraid of some of them
'ere shooting irons, such as your troopers wear on training days. Now,
I'm a true born Yankee American son of liberty, and I never was afraid
of a gun yet in all my life.

JENNY
Well, Mr. Jonathan, you were certainly at the play-house.

JONATHAN
I at the play-house!--Why didn't I see the play then?

JENNY
Why, the people you saw were players.

JONATHAN
Mercy on my soul! did I see the wicked players?-- Mayhap that 'ere

Darby that I liked so was the old serpent himself, and had his cloven
foot in his pocket. Why, I vow, now I come to think on't, the candles
seemed to burn blue, and I am sure where I sat it smelt tarnally of
brimstone.

JESSAMY
Well, Mr. Jonathan, from your account, which I confess is very
accurate, you must have been at the play-house.

JONATHAN
Why, I vow, I began to smell a rat. When I came away, I went to the
man for my money again; you want your money? says he; yes, says I; for
what? says he; why, says I, no man shall jocky me out of my money; I
paid my money to see sights, and the dogs a bit of a sight have I seen,
unless you call listening to people's private business a sight. Why,
says he, it is the School for Scandalization.--The School for
Scandalization!--Oh! ho! no wonder you New-York folks are so cute at
it, when you go to school to learn it; and so I jogged off.

JESSAMY
My dear Jenny, my master's business drags me from you; would to heaven
I knew no other servitude than to your charms.

JONATHAN
Well, but don't go; you won't leave me so--

JESSAMY
Excuse me.--Remember the cash.
[Aside to him, and--Exit.]

JENNY
Mr. Jonathan, won't you please to sit down? Mr. Jessamy tells me you
wanted to have some conversation with me. [Having brought forward two
chairs, they sit.]

JONATHAN
Ma'am!--

JENNY
Sir!--

JONATHAN
Ma'am!--

JENNY
Pray, how do you like the city, Sir?

JONATHAN
Ma'am!--

JENNY
I say, Sir, how do you like New-York?

JONATHAN
Ma'am!--

JENNY

The stupid creature! but I must pass some little time with him, if it is only to endeavour to learn whether it was his master that made such an abrupt entrance into our house, and my young mistress's heart, this morning. [Aside.] As you don't seem to like to talk, Mr. Jonathan--do you sing?

JONATHAN Gor, I--I am glad she asked that, for I forgot what Mr. Jessamy bid me say, and I dare as well be hanged as act what he bid me do, I'm so ashamed. [Aside.] Yes, Ma'am, I can sing--I can sing Mear, Old Hundred, and Bangor.

JENNY

Oh! I don't mean psalm tunes. Have you no little song to please the ladies, such as Roslin Castle, or the Maid of the Mill?

JONATHAN

Why, all my tunes go to meeting tunes, save one, and I count you won't altogether like that 'ere.

JENNY

What is it called?

JONATHAN

I am sure you have heard folks talk about it; it is called Yankee Doodle.

JENNY

Oh! it is the tune I am fond of; and if I know anything of my mistress, she would be glad to dance to it. Pray, sing!

JONATHAN [Sings.]

Father and I went up to camp,
Along with Captain Goodwin;
And there we saw the men and boys,
As thick as hasty-pudding.
Yankee doodle do, etc.

And there we saw a swamping gun,
Big as log of maple,
On a little deuced cars,
A load for father's cattle.
Yankee doodle do, etc.
And every time they fired it off
It took a horn of powder,
It made a noise--like father's gun,
Only a nation louder.
Yankee doodle do, etc.

There was a man in our town,
His name was--

No, no, that won't do. Now, if I was with Tabitha Wymen and Jemima Cawley down at father Chase's, I shouldn't mind singing this all out before them--you would be affronted if I was to sing that, though that's a lucky thought; if you should be affronted, I have something dang'd cute, which Jessamy told me to say to you.

JENNY
Is that all! I assure you I like it of all things.

JONATHAN
No, no; I can sing more; some other time, when you and I are better
acquainted, I'll sing the whole of it--no, no--that's a fib--I can't
sing but a hundred and ninety verses; our Tabitha at home can sing it
all.--[Sings.]

  Marblehead's a rocky place,
  And Cape-Cod is sandy;
  Charlestown is burnt down,
  Boston is the dandy.
  Yankee doodle, doodle do, etc.

I vow, my own town song has put me into such topping spirits that I
believe I'll begin to do a little, as Jessamy says we must when we go
a-courting.--[Runs and kisses her.] Burning rivers! cooling flames!
red-hot roses! pig-nuts! hasty-pudding and ambrosia!

JENNY
What means this freedom? you insulting wretch. [Strikes him.]

JONATHAN
Are you affronted?

JENNY
Affronted! with what looks shall I express my anger?

JONATHAN
Looks! why as to the matter of looks, you look as cross as a witch.

JENNY
Have you no feeling for the delicacy of my sex?

JONATHAN
Feeling! Gor, I--I feel the delicacy of your sex pretty smartly [rubbing his cheek], though, I vow, I thought when you city ladies courted and married, and all that, you put feeling out of the question. But I want to know whether you are really affronted, or only pretend to be so? 'Cause, if you are certainly right down affronted, I am at the end of my tether; Jessamy didn't tell me what to say to you.

JENNY
Pretend to be affronted!

JONATHAN
Aye, aye, if you only pretend, you shall hear how I'll go to work to make cherubim consequences. [Runs up to her.]

JENNY
Begone, you brute!

JONATHAN
That looks like mad; but I won't lose my speech. My dearest Jenny--your name is Jenny, I think?--My dearest Jenny, though I have the highest esteem for the sweet favours you have just now granted

me--Gor, that's a fib, though; but Jessamy says it is not wicked to tell lies to the women. [Aside.] I say, though I have the highest esteem for the favours you have just now granted me, yet you will consider that, as soon as the dissolvable knot is tied, they will no longer be favours, but only matters of duty and matters of course.

JENNY

Marry you! you audacious monster! get out of my sight, or, rather, let me fly from you. [Exit hastily.]

JONATHAN

Gor! she's gone off in a swinging passion, before I had time to think of consequences. If this is the way with your city ladies, give me the twenty acres of rock, the Bible, the cow, and Tabitha, and a little peaceable bundling.

SCENE II. The Mall.

Enter MANLY.

It must be so, Montague! and it is not all the tribe of Mandevilles that shall convince me that a nation, to become great, must first become dissipated. Luxury is surely the bane of a nation: Luxury! which enervates both soul and body, by opening a thousand new sources of enjoyment, opens, also, a thousand new sources of contention and want: Luxury! which renders a people weak at home, and accessible to bribery, corruption, and force from abroad. When the Grecian states knew no other tools than the axe and the saw, the Grecians were a great, a free, and a happy people. The kings of Greece devoted their lives to the service of their country, and her senators knew no other superiority over their fellow-citizens than a glorious pre-eminence in danger and virtue. They exhibited to the world a noble spectacle,--a number of independent states united by a similarity of language, sentiment, manners, common interest, and common consent, in one grand mutual league of protection. And, thus united, long might they have continued the cherishers of arts and sciences, the protectors of the oppressed, the scourge of tyrants, and the safe asylum of liberty. But when foreign gold, and still more pernicious foreign luxury, had crept among them, they sapped the vitals of their virtue. The virtues of their ancestors were only found in their writings. Envy and suspicion, the vices of little minds, possessed them. The various states engendered jealousies of each other; and, more unfortunately, growing jealous of their great federal council, the Amphictyons, they forgot that their common safety had existed, and would exist, in giving them an honourable extensive prerogative. The common good was lost in the pursuit of private interest; and that people who, by uniting, might have stood against the world in arms, by dividing, crumbled into ruin;--their name is now only known in the page of the historian, and what they once were is all we have left to admire. Oh! that America! Oh! that my country, would, in this her day, learn the things which belong to her peace!

Enter DIMPLE.

DIMPLE
You are Colonel Manly, I presume?

MANLY
At your service, Sir.

DIMPLE
My name is Dimple, Sir. I have the honour to be a lodger in the same house with you, and, hearing you were in the Mall, came hither to take the liberty of joining you.

MANLY
You are very obliging, Sir.

DIMPLE
As I understand you are a stranger here, Sir, I have taken the liberty to introduce myself to your acquaintance, as possibly I may have it in my power to point out some things in this city worthy your notice.

MANLY An attention to strangers is worthy a liberal mind, and must ever be gratefully received. But to a soldier, who has no fixed abode, such attentions are particularly pleasing.

DIMPLE
Sir, there is no character so respectable as that of a soldier. And, indeed, when we reflect how much we owe to those brave men who have suffered so much in the service of their country, and secured to us those inestimable blessings that we now enjoy, our liberty and independence, they demand every attention which gratitude can pay. For my own part, I never meet an officer, but I embrace him as my friend, nor a private in distress, but I insensibly extend my charity to him.--I have hit the Bumkin off very tolerably.

[Aside.

MANLY

Give me your hand, Sir! I do not proffer this hand to everybody; but
you steal into my heart. I hope I am as insensible to flattery as most
men; but I declare (it may be my weak side) that I never hear the name
of soldier mentioned with respect, but I experience a thrill of
pleasure which I never feel on any other occasion.

DIMPLE

Will you give me leave, my dear Colonel, to confer an obligation on
myself, by shewing you some civilities during your stay here, and
giving a similar opportunity to some of my friends?

MANLY

Sir, I thank you; but I believe my stay in this city will be very short.

DIMPLE

I can introduce you to some men of excellent sense, in whose company
you will esteem yourself happy; and, by way of amusement, to some fine
girls, who will listen to your soft things with pleasure.

MANLY

Sir, I should be proud of the honour of being acquainted with those
gentlemen;--but, as for the ladies, I don't understand you.

DIMPLE

Why, Sir, I need not tell you, that when a young gentleman is alone
with a young lady he must say some soft things to her fair
cheek--indeed, the lady will expect it. To be sure, there is not much
pleasure when a man of the world and a finished coquette meet, who

perfectly know each other; but how delicious is it to excite the
emotions of joy, hope, expectation, and delight in the bosom of a
lovely girl who believes every tittle of what you say to be serious!

MANLY

Serious, Sir! In my opinion, the man who, under pretensions of
marriage, can plant thorns in the bosom of an innocent, unsuspecting
girl is more detestable than a common robber, in the same proportion as
private violence is more despicable than open force, and money of less
value than happiness.

DIMPLE

How he awes me by the superiority of his sentiments. [Aside.] As you
say, Sir, a gentleman should be cautious how he mentions marriage.

MANLY

Cautious, Sir! No person more approves of an intercourse between the
sexes than I do. Female conversation softens our manners, whilst our
discourse, from the superiority of our literary advantages, improves
their minds. But, in our young country, where there is no such thing
as gallantry, when a gentleman speaks of love to a lady, whether he
mentions marriage or not, she ought to conclude either that he meant to
insult her or that his intentions are the most serious and honourable.
How mean, how cruel, is it, by a thousand tender assiduities, to win
the affections of an amiable girl, and, though you leave her virtue
unspotted, to betray her into the appearance of so many tender
partialities, that every man of delicacy would suppress his inclination
towards her, by supposing her heart engaged! Can any man, for the
trivial gratification of his leisure hours, affect the happiness of a
whole life! His not having spoken of marriage may add to his perfidy,

but can be no excuse for his conduct.

DIMPLE
Sir, I admire your sentiments;--they are mine. The light observations
that fell from me were only a principle of the tongue; they came not
from the heart; my practice has ever disapproved these principles.

MANLY
I believe you, Sir. I should with reluctance suppose that those
pernicious sentiments could find admittance into the heart of a
gentleman.

DIMPLE
I am now, Sir, going to visit a family, where, if you please, I will
have the honour of introducing you. Mr. Manly's ward, Miss Letitia, is
a young lady of immense fortune; and his niece, Miss Charlotte Manly,
is a young lady of great sprightliness and beauty.

MANLY
That gentleman, Sir, is my uncle, and Miss Manly my sister.

DIMPLE
The devil she is! [Aside.] Miss Manly your sister, Sir? I rejoice to
hear it, and feel a double pleasure in being known to you.--Plague on
him! I wish he was at Boston again, with all my soul. [Aside.]

MANLY
Come, Sir, will you go?

DIMPLE
I will follow you in a moment, Sir. [Exit Manly.] Plague on it! this
is unlucky. A fighting brother is a cursed appendage to a fine girl.
Egad! I just stopped in time; had he not discovered himself, in two
minutes more I should have told him how well I was with his sister.
Indeed, I cannot see the satisfaction of an intrigue, if one can't have
the pleasure of communicating it to our friends.   [Exit.

END OF THE THIRD ACT.

ACT IV.

SCENE I.

CHARLOTTE'S Apartment.

CHARLOTTE leading in MARIA.

CHARLOTTE
THIS is so kind, my sweet friend, to come to see me at this moment. I declare, if I were going to be married in a few days, as you are, I should scarce have found time to visit my friends.

MARIA
Do you think, then, that there is an impropriety in it?--How should you dispose of your time?

CHARLOTTE
Why, I should be shut up in my chamber; and my head would so run upon--upon--upon the solemn ceremony that I was to pass through!--I declare, it would take me above two hours merely to learn that little monosyllable--Yes. Ah! my dear, your sentimental imagination does not

conceive what that little tiny word implies.

MARIA Spare me your raillery, my sweet friend; I should love your
agreeable vivacity at any other time.

CHARLOTTE
Why, this is the very time to amuse you. You grieve me to see you look
so unhappy.

MARIA
Have I not reason to look so?

CHARLOTTE
What new grief distresses you?

MARIA
Oh! how sweet it is, when the heart is borne down with misfortune, to
recline and repose on the bosom of friendship! Heaven knows that,
although it is improper for a young lady to praise a gentleman, yet I
have ever concealed Mr. Dimple's foibles, and spoke of him as of one
whose reputation I expected would be linked with mine; but his late
conduct towards me has turned my coolness into contempt. He behaves as
if he meant to insult and disgust me; whilst my father, in the last
conversation on the subject of our marriage, spoke of it as a matter
which lay near his heart, and in which he would not bear contradiction.

CHARLOTTE

This works well; oh! the generous Dimple. I'll endeavour to excite her
to discharge him. [Aside.] But, my dear friend, your happiness depends
on yourself. Why don't you discard him? Though the match has been of
long standing, I would not be forced to make myself miserable: no
parent in the world should oblige me to marry the man I did not like.

MARIA

Oh! my dear, you never lived with your parents, and do not know what
influence a father's frowns have upon a daughter's heart. Besides,
what have I to alledge against Mr. Dimple, to justify myself to the
world? He carries himself so smoothly, that every one would impute the
blame to me, and call me capricious.

CHARLOTTE

And call her capricious! Did ever such an objection start into the
heart of woman? For my part, I wish I had fifty lovers to discard, for
no other reason than because I did not fancy them. My dear Maria, you
will forgive me; I know your candour and confidence in me; but I have
at times, I confess, been led to suppose that some other gentleman was
the cause of your aversion to Mr. Dimple.

MARIA

No, my sweet friend, you may be assured, that though I have seen many
gentlemen I could prefer to Mr. Dimple, yet I never saw one that I
thought I could give my hand to, until this morning.

CHARLOTTE

This morning!

MARIA

Yes; one of the strangest accidents in the world. The odious Dimple, after disgusting me with his conversation, had just left me, when a gentleman, who, it seems, boards in the same house with him, saw him coming out of our door, and, the houses looking very much alike, he came into our house instead of his lodgings; nor did he discover his mistake until he got into the parlour, where I was; he then bowed so gracefully, made such a genteel apology, and looked so manly and noble!--

CHARLOTTE

I see some folks, though it is so great an impropriety, can praise a gentleman, when he happens to be the man of their fancy. [Aside.]

MARIA

I don't know how it was,--I hope he did not think me indelicate,--but I asked him, I believe, to sit down, or pointed to a chair. He sat down, and, instead of having recourse to observations upon the weather, or hackneyed criticisms upon the theatre, he entered readily into a conversation worthy a man of sense to speak, and a lady of delicacy and sentiment to hear. He was not strictly handsome, but he spoke the language of sentiment, and his eyes looked tenderness and honour.

CHARLOTTE

Oh! [eagerly] you sentimental, grave girls, when your hearts are once touched, beat us rattles a bar's length. And so you are quite in love with this he-angel?

MARIA

In love with him! How can you rattle so, Charlotte? am I not going to be miserable? [Sighs.] In love with a gentleman I never saw but one hour in my life, and don't know his name! No; I only wished that the man I shall marry may look, and talk, and act, just like him. Besides, my dear, he is a married man.

CHARLOTTE

Why, that was good-natured--he told you so, I suppose, in mere charity, to prevent you falling in love with him?

MARIA

He didn't tell me so; [peevishly] he looked as if he was married.

CHARLOTTE

How, my dear; did he look sheepish?

MARIA

I am sure he has a susceptible heart, and the ladies of his acquaintance must be very stupid not to--

CHARLOTTE

Hush! I hear some person coming.

Enter LETITIA.

LETITIA
My dear Maria, I am happy to see you. Lud! what a pity it is that you have purchased your wedding clothes.

MARIA
I think so. [Sighing.]

LETITIA
Why, my dear, there is the sweetest parcel of silks come over you ever saw! Nancy Brilliant has a full suit come; she sent over her measure, and it fits her to a hair; it is immensely dressy, and made for a court-hoop. I thought they said the large hoops were going out of fashion.

CHARLOTTE
Did you see the hat? Is it a fact that the deep laces round the border is still the fashion?

DIMPLE within. Upon my honour, Sir.

MARIA
Ha! Dimple's voice! My dear, I must take leave of you. There are some things necessary to be done at our house. Can't I go through the other room?

Enter DIMPLE and MANLY.

DIMPLE
Ladies, your most obedient.

CHARLOTTE
Miss Van Rough, shall I present my brother Henry to you? Colonel
Manly, Maria,--Miss Van Rough, brother.

MARIA
Her brother! [turns and sees Manly.] Oh! my heart! the very gentleman
I have been praising.

MANLY
The same amiable girl I saw this morning!

CHARLOTTE
Why, you look as if you were acquainted.

MANLY
I unintentionally intruded into this lady's presence this morning, for
which she was so good as to promise me her forgiveness.

CHARLOTTE
Oh! ho! is that the case! Have these two penserosos been together?
Were they Henry's eyes that looked so tenderly? [Aside.] And so you
promised to pardon him? and could you be so good-natured? have you
really forgiven him? I beg you would do it for my sake [whispering
loud to Maria]. But, my dear, as you are in such haste, it would be

cruel to detain you; I can show you the way through the other room.

MARIA
Spare me, my sprightly friend.

MANLY The lady does not, I hope, intend to deprive us of the pleasure
of her company so soon.

CHARLOTTE
She has only a mantua-maker who waits for her at home. But, as I am to
give my opinion of the dress, I think she cannot go yet. We were
talking of the fashions when you came in, but I suppose the subject
must be changed to something of more importance now. Mr. Dimple, will
you favour us with an account of the public entertainments?

DIMPLE
Why, really, Miss Manly, you could not have asked me a question more
mal-apropos. For my part, I must confess that, to a man who has
travelled, there is nothing that is worthy the name of amusement to be
found in this city.

CHARLOTTE
Except visiting the ladies.

DIMPLE
Pardon me, Madam; that is the avocation of a man of taste. But for
amusement, I positively know of nothing that can be called so, unless

you dignify with that title the hopping once a fortnight to the sound of two or three squeaking fiddles, and the clattering of the old tavern windows, or sitting to see the miserable mummers, whom you call actors, murder comedy and make a farce of tragedy.

MANLY
Do you never attend the theatre, Sir?

DIMPLE
I was tortured there once.

CHARLOTTE Pray, Mr. Dimple, was it a tragedy or a comedy?

DIMPLE
Faith, Madam, I cannot tell; for I sat with my back to the stage all the time, admiring a much better actress than any there--a lady who played the fine woman to perfection; though, by the laugh of the horrid creatures round me, I suppose it was comedy. Yet, on second thoughts, it might be some hero in a tragedy, dying so comically as to set the whole house in an uproar. Colonel, I presume you have been in Europe?

MANLY
Indeed, Sir, I was never ten leagues from the continent.

DIMPLE
Believe me, Colonel, you have an immense pleasure to come; and when you shall have seen the brilliant exhibitions of Europe, you will learn to despise the amusements of this country as much as I do.

MANLY

Therefore I do not wish to see them; for I can never esteem that
knowledge valuable which tends to give me a distaste for my native
country.

DIMPLE

Well, Colonel, though you have not travelled, you have read.

MANLY

I have, a little; and by it have discovered that there is a laudable
partiality which ignorant, untravelled men entertain for everything
that belongs to their native country. I call it laudable; it injures
no one; adds to their own happiness; and, when extended, becomes the
noble principle of patriotism. Travelled gentlemen rise superior, in
their own opinion, to this; but if the contempt which they contract for
their country is the most valuable acquisition of their travels, I am
far from thinking that their time and money are well spent.

MARIA

What noble sentiments!

CHARLOTTE

Let my brother set out where he will in the fields of conversation, he
is sure to end his tour in the temple of gravity.

MANLY

Forgive me, my sister. I love my country; it has its foibles
undoubtedly;--some foreigners will with pleasure remark them--but such
remarks fall very ungracefully from the lips of her citizens.

DIMPLE
You are perfectly in the right, Colonel--America has her faults.

MANLY
Yes, Sir; and we, her children, should blush for them in private, and endeavour, as individuals, to reform them. But, if our country has its errors in common with other countries, I am proud to say America--I mean the United States--has displayed virtues and achievements which modern nations may admire, but of which they have seldom set us the example.

CHARLOTTE
But, brother, we must introduce you to some of our gay folks, and let you see the city, such as it is. Mr. Dimple is known to almost every family in town; he will doubtless take a pleasure in introducing you.

DIMPLE
I shall esteem every service I can render your brother an honour.

MANLY
I fear the business I am upon will take up all my time, and my family will be anxious to hear from me.

MARIA
His family! but what is it to me that he is married! [Aside.] Pray, how did you leave your lady, Sir?

CHARLOTTE
My brother is not married [observing her anxiety]; it is only an odd
way he has of expressing himself. Pray, brother, is this business,
which you make your continual excuse, a secret?

MANLY
No, sister; I came hither to solicit the honourable Congress, that a
number of my brave old soldiers may be put upon the pension-list, who
were, at first, not judged to be so materially wounded as to need the
public assistance. My sister says true [to Maria]: I call my late
soldiers my family. Those who were not in the field in the late
glorious contest, and those who were, have their respective merits;
but, I confess, my old brother-soldiers are dearer to me than the
former description. Friendships made in adversity are lasting; our
countrymen may forget us, but that is no reason why we should forget
one another. But I must leave you; my time of engagement approaches.

CHARLOTTE
Well, but, brother, if you will go, will you please to conduct my fair
friend home? You live in the same street--I was to have gone with her
myself-- [Aside]. A lucky thought.

MARIA I am obliged to your sister, Sir, and was just intending to go.
[Going.]

MANLY
I shall attend her with pleasure. [Exit with Maria, followed by Dimple
and Charlotte.]

MARIA
Now, pray, don't betray me to your brother.

CHARLOTTE
[Just as she sees him make a motion to take his leave.] One word with you, brother, if you please. [Follows them out.

Manent, DIMPLE and LETITIA.

DIMPLE
You received the billet I sent you, I presume?

LETITIA
Hush!--Yes.

DIMPLE
When shall I pay my respects to you?

LETITIA
At eight I shall be unengaged.

Reenter CHARLOTTE.

DIMPLE
Did my lovely angel receive my billet? [to Charlotte.]

CHARLOTTE
Yes.

DIMPLE
At eight I shall be at home unengaged.

DIMPLE
Unfortunate! I have a horrid engagement of business at that hour.
Can't you finish your visit earlier and let six be the happy hour?

CHARLOTTE
You know your influence over me. [Exeunt severally.

SCENE II.

VAN ROUGH'S House.

VAN ROUGH, alone.

IT cannot possibly be true! The son of my old friend can't have acted
so unadvisedly. Seventeen thousand pounds! in bills! Mr. Transfer
must have been mistaken. He always appeared so prudent, and talked so
well upon money matters, and even assured me that he intended to change
his dress for a suit of clothes which would not cost so much, and look
more substantial, as soon as he married. No, no, no! it can't be; it
cannot be. But, however, I must look out sharp. I did not care what
his principles or his actions were, so long as he minded the main
chance. Seventeen thousand pounds! If he had lost it in trade, why
the best men may have ill-luck; but to game it away, as Transfer
says--why, at this rate, his whole estate may go in one night, and,
what is ten times worse, mine into the bargain. No, no; Mary is right.
Leave women to look out in these matters; for all they look as if they
didn't know a journal from a ledger, when their interest is concerned
they know what's what; they mind the main chance as well as the best of
us. I wonder Mary did not tell me she knew of his spending his money
so foolishly. Seventeen thousand pounds! Why, if my daughter was
standing up to be married, I would forbid the banns, if I found it was
to a man who did not mind the main chance.--Hush! I hear somebody
coming. 'Tis Mary's voice; a man with her too! I shouldn't be
surprised if this should be the other string to her bow. Aye, aye, let
them alone; women understand the main chance.--Though, I' faith, I'll
listen a little.   [Retires into a closet.

MANLY leading in MARIA.

MANLY
I hope you will excuse my speaking upon so important a subject so
abruptly; but, the moment I entered your room, you struck me as the
lady whom I had long loved in imagination, and never hoped to see.

MARIA
Indeed, Sir, I have been led to hear more upon this subject than I
ought.

MANLY
Do you, then, disapprove my suit, Madam, or the abruptness of my
introducing it? If the latter, my peculiar situation, being obliged to
leave the city in a few days, will, I hope, be my excuse; if the
former, I will retire, for I am sure I would not give a moment's
inquietude to her whom I could devote my life to please. I am not so
indelicate as to seek your immediate approbation; permit me only to be
near you, and by a thousand tender assiduities to endeavour to excite a
grateful return.

MARIA
I have a father, whom I would die to make happy; he will disapprove--

MANLY
Do you think me so ungenerous as to seek a place in your esteem without
his consent? You must--you ever ought to consider that man as unworthy
of you who seeks an interest in your heart contrary to a father's

approbation. A young lady should reflect that the loss of a lover may be supplied, but nothing can compensate for the loss of a parent's affection. Yet, why do you suppose your father would disapprove? In our country, the affections are not sacrificed to riches or family aggrandizement: should you approve, my family is decent, and my rank honourable.

MARIA
You distress me, Sir.

MANLY
Then I will sincerely beg your excuse for obtruding so disagreeable a subject, and retire.   [Going.

MARIA
Stay, Sir! your generosity and good opinion of me deserve a return; but why must I declare what, for these few hours, I have scarce suffered myself to think?--I am--

MANLY
What?

MARIA
Engaged, Sir; and, in a few days, to be married to the gentleman you saw at your sister's.

MANLY

Engaged to be married! And have I been basely invading the rights of another? Why have you permitted this? Is this the return for the partiality I declared for you?

MARIA

You distress me, Sir. What would you have me say? You are too generous to wish the truth. Ought I to say that I dared not suffer myself to think of my engagement, and that I am going to give my hand without my heart? Would you have me confess a partiality for you? If so, your triumph is compleat, and can be only more so when days of misery with the man I cannot love will make me think of him whom I could prefer.

MANLY [after a pause].

We are both unhappy; but it is your duty to obey your parent--mine to obey my honour. Let us, therefore, both follow the path of rectitude; and of this we may be assured, that if we are not happy, we shall, at least, deserve to be so. Adieu! I dare not trust myself longer with you.   [Exeunt severally.

END OF THE FOURTH ACT.

ACT V.

SCENE I.

DIMPLE'S Lodgings.

JESSAMY meeting JONATHAN.

JESSAMY
WELL, Mr. Jonathan, what success with the fair?

JONATHAN
Why, such a tarnal cross tike you never saw! You would have counted she had lived upon crab-apples and vinegar for a fortnight. But what the rattle makes you look so tarnation glum?

JESSAMY
I was thinking, Mr. Jonathan, what could be the reason of her carrying herself so coolly to you.

JONATHAN
Coolly, do you call it? Why, I vow, she was fire-hot angry: may be it

was because I buss'd her.

JESSAMY
No, no, Mr. Jonathan; there must be some other cause; I never yet knew a lady angry at being kissed.

JONATHAN
Well, if it is not the young woman's bashfulness, I vow I can't conceive why she shouldn't like me.

JESSAMY
May be it is because you have not the Graces, Mr. Jonathan.

JONATHAN
Grace! Why, does the young woman expect I must be converted before I court her?

JESSAMY
I mean graces of person: for instance, my lord tells us that we must cut off our nails even at top, in small segments of circles--though you won't understand that; in the next place, you must regulate your laugh.

JONATHAN
Maple-log seize it! don't I laugh natural?

JESSAMY
That's the very fault, Mr. Jonathan. Besides, you absolutely misplace it. I was told by a friend of mine that you laughed outright at the play the other night, when you ought only to have tittered.

JONATHAN
Gor! I--what does one go to see fun for if they can't laugh?

JESSAMY You may laugh; but you must laugh by rule.

JONATHAN
Swamp it--laugh by rule! Well, I should like that tarnally.

JESSAMY
Why, you know, Mr. Jonathan, that to dance, a lady to play with her fan, or a gentleman with his cane, and all other natural motions, are regulated by art. My master has composed an immensely pretty gamut, by which any lady or gentleman, with a few years' close application, may learn to laugh as gracefully as if they were born and bred to it.

JONATHAN
Mercy on my soul! A gamut for laughing--just like fa, la, sol?

JEREMY
Yes. It comprises every possible display of jocularity, from an affettuoso smile to a piano titter, or full chorus fortissimo ha, ha, ha! My master employs his leisure hours in marking out the plays, like

a cathedral chanting-book, that the ignorant may know where to laugh; and that pit, box, and gallery may keep time together, and not have a snigger in one part of the house, a broad grin in the other, and a d---d grum look in the third. How delightful to see the audience all smile together, then look on their books, then twist their mouths into an agreeable simper, then altogether shake the house with a general ha, ha, ha! loud as a full chorus of Handel's at an Abbey commemoration.

JONATHAN
Ha, ha, ha! that's dang'd cute, I swear.

JESSAMY
The gentlemen, you see, will laugh the tenor; the ladies will play the counter-tenor; the beaux will squeak the treble; and our jolly friends in the gallery a thorough base, ho, ho, ho!

JONATHAN
Well, can't you let me see that gamut?

JESSAMY
Oh! yes, Mr. Jonathan; here it is. [Takes out a book.] Oh! no, this is only a titter with its variations. Ah, here it is. [Takes out another.] Now, you must know, Mr. Jonathan, this is a piece written by Ben Johnson, which I have set to my master's gamut. The places where you must smile, look grave, or laugh outright, are marked below the line. Now look over me. "There was a certain man"--now you must smile.

JONATHAN

Well, read it again; I warrant I'll mind my eye.

JESSAMY

"There was a certain man, who had a sad scolding wife,"--now you must laugh.

JONATHAN

Tarnation! That's no laughing matter though.

JESSAMY

"And she lay sick a-dying";--now you must titter.

JONATHAN

What, snigger when the good woman's a-dying! Gor, I--

JESSAMY

Yes, the notes say you must--"and she asked her husband leave to make a will,"--now you must begin to look grave;--"and her husband said"--

JONATHAN

Ay, what did her husband say? Something dang'd cute, I reckon.

JESSAMY

"And her husband said, you have had your will all your life-time, and would you have it after you are dead, too?"

JONATHAN

Ho, ho, ho! There the old man was even with her; he was up to the notch--ha, ha, ha!

JESSAMY

But, Mr. Jonathan, you must not laugh so. Why you ought to have tittered piano, and you have laughed fortissimo. Look here; you see these marks, A, B, C, and so on; these are the references to the other part of the book. Let us turn to it, and you will see the directions how to manage the muscles. This [turns over] was note D you blundered at.--You must purse the mouth into a smile, then titter, discovering the lower part of the three front upper teeth.

JONATHAN

How? read it again.

JESSAMY

"There was a certain man"--very well!--"who had a sad scolding wife,"--why don't you laugh?

JONATHAN

Now, that scolding wife sticks in my gizzard so pluckily that I can't laugh for the blood and nowns of me. Let me look grave here, and I'll laugh your belly full, where the old creature's a-dying.

JESSAMY

"And she asked her husband"--[Bell rings.] My master's bell! he's returned, I fear.--Here, Mr. Jonathan, take this gamut; and I make no doubt but with a few years' close application, you may be able to smile gracefully."

[Exeunt severally.

SCENE II.

CHARLOTTE'S Apartment.

Enter MANLY.

MANLY
WHAT, no one at home? How unfortunate to meet the only lady my heart was ever moved by, to find her engaged to another, and confessing her partiality for me! Yet engaged to a man who, by her intimation, and his libertine conversation with me, I fear, does not merit her. Aye! there's the sting; for, were I assured that Maria was happy, my heart is not so selfish but that it would dilate in knowing it, even though it were with another. But to know she is unhappy!--I must drive these thoughts from me. Charlotte has some books; and this is what I believe she calls her little library.   [Enters a closet.

Enter DIMPLE leading LETITIA.

LETITIA
And will you pretend to say now, Mr. Dimple, that you propose to break with Maria? Are not the banns published? Are not the clothes purchased? Are not the friends invited? In short, is it not a done affair?

DIMPLE
Believe me, my dear Letitia, I would not marry her.

LETITIA
Why have you not broke with her before this, as you all along deluded me by saying you would?

DIMPLE
Because I was in hopes she would, ere this, have broke with me.

LETITIA
You could not expect it.

DIMPLE
Nay, but be calm a moment; 'twas from my regard to you that I did not discard her.

LETITIA
Regard to me!

DIMPLE
Yes; I have done everything in my power to break with her, but the foolish girl is so fond of me that nothing can accomplish it. Besides, how can I offer her my hand when my heart is indissolubly engaged to you?

LETITIA
There may be reason in this; but why so attentive to Miss Manly?

DIMPLE
Attentive to Miss Manly! For heaven's sake, if you have no better opinion of my constancy, pay not so ill a compliment to my taste.

LETITIA
Did I not see you whisper her to-day?

DIMPLE
Possibly I might--but something of so very trifling a nature that I have already forgot what it was.

LETITIA
I believe she has not forgot it.

DIMPLE
My dear creature, how can you for a moment suppose I should have any serious thoughts of that trifling, gay, flighty coquette, that disagreeable--

Enter CHARLOTTE.

DIMPLE
My dear Miss Manly, I rejoice to see you; there is a charm in your
conversation that always marks your entrance into company as fortunate.

LETITIA
Where have you been, my dear?

CHARLOTTE
Why, I have been about to twenty shops, turning over pretty things, and
so have left twenty visits unpaid. I wish you would step into the
carriage and whisk round, make my apology, and leave my cards where our
friends are not at home; that, you know, will serve as a visit. Come,
do go.

LETITIA
So anxious to get me out! but I'll watch you. [Aside.] Oh! yes, I'll
go; I want a little exercise. Positively [Dimple offering to accompany
her], Mr. Dimple, you shall not go; why, half my visits are cake and
caudle visits; it won't do, you know, for you to go. [Exit, but
returns to the door in the back scene and listens.]

DIMPLE
This attachment of your brother to Maria is fortunate.

CHARLOTTE
How did you come to the knowledge of it?

DIMPLE
I read it in their eyes.

CHARLOTTE
And I had it from her mouth. It would have amused you to have seen her! She, that thought it so great an impropriety to praise a gentleman that she could not bring out one word in your favour, found a redundancy to praise him.

DIMPLE
I have done everything in my power to assist his passion there: your delicacy, my dearest girl, would be shocked at half the instances of neglect and misbehaviour.

CHARLOTTE
I don't know how I should bear neglect; but Mr. Dimple must misbehave himself indeed, to forfeit my good opinion.

DIMPLE
Your good opinion, my angel, is the pride and pleasure of my heart; and if the most respectful tenderness for you, and an utter indifference for all your sex besides, can make me worthy of your esteem, I shall richly merit it.

CHARLOTTE
All my sex besides, Mr. Dimple!--you forgot your tete-a-tete with Letitia.

DIMPLE
How can you, my lovely angel, cast a thought on that insipid, wry-mouthed, ugly creature!

CHARLOTTE
But her fortune may have charms?

DIMPLE
Not to a heart like mine. The man, who has been blessed with the good opinion of my Charlotte, must despise the allurements of fortune.

CHARLOTTE
I am satisfied.

DIMPLE
Let us think no more on the odious subject, but devote the present hour to happiness.

CHARLOTTE
Can I be happy when I see the man I prefer going to be married to another?

DIMPLE
Have I not already satisfied my charming angel, that I can never think
of marrying the puling Maria? But, even if it were so, could that be
any bar to our happiness? for, as the poet sings,

  "Love, free as air, at sight of human ties,
  Spreads his light wings, and in a moment flies."

Come, then, my charming angel! why delay our bliss? The present moment
is ours; the next is in the hand of fate. [Kissing her.]

CHARLOTTE
Begone, Sir! By your delusions you had almost lulled my honour asleep.

DIMPLE
Let me lull the demon to sleep again with kisses. [He struggles with
her; she screams.]

Enter MANLY.

MANLY
Turn, villain! and defend yourself.--[Draws.]

[VAN ROUGH enters and beats down their swords.]

VAN ROUGH
Is the devil in you? are you going to murder one another? [Holding

Dimple.]

DIMPLE
Hold him, hold him,--I can command my passion.

Enter JONATHAN.

JONATHAN
What the rattle ails you? Is the old one in you? Let the colonel
alone, can't you? I feel chock-full of fight,--do you want to kill the
colonel?--

MANLY
Be still, Jonathan; the gentleman does not want to hurt me.

JONATHAN
Gor! I--I wish he did; I'd shew him Yankee boys play, pretty
quick.--Don't you see you have frightened the young woman into the
hystrikes?

VAN ROUGH
Pray, some of you explain this; what has been the occasion of all this
racket?

MANLY
That gentleman can explain it to you; it will be a very diverting story
for an intended father-in-law to hear.

VAN ROUGH
How was this matter, Mr. Van Dumpling?

DIMPLE
Sir,--upon my honour,--all I know is, that I was talking to this young
lady, and this gentleman broke in on us in a very extraordinary manner.

VAN ROUGH
Why, all this is nothing to the purpose; can you explain it, Miss? [To
Charlotte.]

Enter LETITIA through the back scene.

LETITIA
I can explain it to that gentleman's confusion. Though long betrothed
to your daughter [to Van Rough], yet, allured by my fortune, it seems
(with shame do I speak it) he has privately paid his addresses to me.
I was drawn in to listen to him by his assuring me that the match was
made by his father without his consent, and that he proposed to break
with Maria, whether he married me or not. But, whatever were his
intentions respecting your daughter, Sir, even to me he was false; for
he has repeated the same story, with some cruel reflections upon my
person, to Miss Manly.

JONATHAN
What a tarnal curse!

LETITIA
Nor is this all, Miss Manly. When he was with me this very morning, he
made the same ungenerous reflections upon the weakness of your mind as
he has so recently done upon the defects of my person.

JONATHAN
What a tarnal curse and damn, too!

DIMPLE
Ha! since I have lost Letitia, I believe I had as good make it up with
Maria. Mr. Van Rough, at present I cannot enter into particulars; but,
I believe, I can explain everything to your satisfaction in private.

VAN ROUGH
There is another matter, Mr. Van Dumpling, which I would have you
explain. Pray, Sir, have Messrs. Van Cash & Co. presented you those
bills for acceptance?

DIMPLE
The deuce! Has he heard of those bills! Nay, then, all's up with
Maria, too; but an affair of this sort can never prejudice me among the
ladies; they will rather long to know what the dear creature possesses
to make him so agreeable. [Aside.] Sir, you'll hear from me. [To
Manly.]

MANLY
And you from me, Sir--

DIMPLE
Sir, you wear a sword--

MANLY
Yes, Sir. This sword was presented to me by that brave Gallic hero, the Marquis De la Fayette. I have drawn it in the service of my country, and in private life, on the only occasion where a man is justified in drawing his sword, in defence of a lady's honour. I have fought too many battles in the service of my country to dread the imputation of cowardice. Death from a man of honour would be a glory you do not merit; you shall live to bear the insult of man and the contempt of that sex whose general smiles afforded you all your happiness.

DIMPLE
You won't meet me, Sir? Then I'll post you for a coward.

MANLY I'll venture that, Sir. The reputation of my life does not depend upon the breath of a Mr. Dimple. I would have you to know, however, Sir, that I have a cane to chastise the insolence of a scoundrel, and a sword and the good laws of my country to protect me from the attempts of an assassin--

DIMPLE
Mighty well! Very fine, indeed! Ladies and gentlemen, I take my leave; and you will please to observe in the case of my deportment the contrast between a gentleman who has read Chesterfield and received the polish of Europe and an unpolished, untravelled American.
[Exit.

Enter MARIA.

MARIA
Is he indeed gone?--

LETITIA
I hope, never to return.

VAN ROUGH
I am glad I heard of those bills; though it's plaguy unlucky; I hoped
to see Mary married before I died.

MANLY
Will you permit a gentleman, Sir, to offer himself as a suitor to your
daughter? Though a stranger to you, he is not altogether so to her, or
unknown in this city. You may find a son-in-law of more fortune, but
you can never meet with one who is richer in love for her, or respect
for you.

VAN ROUGH
Why, Mary, you have not let this gentleman make love to you without my
leave?

MANLY
I did not say, Sir--

MARIA
Say, Sir!--I--the gentleman, to be sure, met me accidentally.

VAN ROUGH
Ha, ha, ha! Mark me, Mary; young folks think old folks to be fools;
but old folks know young folks to be fools. Why, I knew all about this
affair. This was only a cunning way I had to bring it about. Hark ye!
I was in the closet when you and he were at our hours. [Turns to the
company.] I heard that little baggage say she loved her old father,
and would die to make him happy! Oh! how I loved the little baggage!
And you talked very prudently, young man. I have inquired into your
character, and find you to be a man of punctuality and mind the main
chance. And so, as you love Mary and Mary loves you, you shall have my
consent immediately to be married. I'll settle my fortune on you, and
go and live with you the remainder of my life.

MANLY
Sir, I hope--

VAN ROUGH
Come, come, no fine speeches; mind the main chance, young man, and you
and I shall always agree.

LETITIA I sincerely wish you joy [advancing to Maria]; and hope your
pardon for my conduct.

MARIA
I thank you for your congratulations, and hope we shall at once forget

the wretch who has given us so much disquiet, and the trouble that he has occasioned.

CHARLOTTE
And I, my dear Maria,--how shall I look up to you for forgiveness? I, who, in the practice of the meanest arts, have violated the most sacred rights of friendship? I can never forgive myself, or hope charity from the world; but, I confess, I have much to hope from such a brother; and I am happy that I may soon say, such a sister.

MARIA
My dear, you distress me; you have all my love.

MANLY
And mine.

CHARLOTTE
If repentance can entitle me to forgiveness, I have already much merit; for I despise the littleness of my past conduct. I now find that the heart of any worthy man cannot be gained by invidious attacks upon the rights and characters of others;--by countenancing the addresses of a thousand;--or that the finest assemblage of features, the greatest taste in dress, the genteelest address, or the most brilliant wit, cannot eventually secure a coquette from contempt and ridicule.

MANLY
And I have learned that probity, virtue, honour, though they should not have received the polish of Europe, will secure to an honest American

---

the good graces of his fair countrywomen, and, I hope, the applause of THE PUBLIC.

NOTES.

[1] In addition to the 'Prince of Parthia,' the following plays by American authors are known to have been printed:

1. 'The Suspected Daughter, or Jealous Father,' a Farce in three acts, both serious and comic, written by T. T. Boston, 1751.

2. 'The Disappointment, or The Force of Credulity,' a new American Comic Opera of two acts, by Andrew Barton, Esq. New-York, 1767.

3. 'The Conquest of Canada, or Siege of Quebec, a Historic Tragedy,' by George Cockings. Philadelphia, 1772.

4. 'The Adulateur,' a tragedy; and

5. 'The Group,' a Political Comedy, 1775; both by Mrs. Mercy Warren.

6. 'The Blockheads, or the Affrighted Officers,' a Farce. Boston, 1776.

7. 'The Battle of Bunker Hill,' a dramatic piece, in five acts. Philadelphia, 1776; and

8. 'The Death of General Montgomery in storming the City of Quebec,' a Tragedy. Philadelphia, 1777; both by H. H. Brackenridge.

9. 'The Patriot Chief,' a Drama, by Peter Markoe. Philadelphia, 1783.

10. 'Edwin and Angelina, or The Banditti,' an Opera in three acts, by Dr. Elihu H. Smith. New-York, 1787.

[2] Dunlap erroneously gives the date of the first performance of the 'Contrast' as in 1786, and writers generally following him make the same mistake. Ireland in his 'Records' gives the date correctly.

[3] Tyler, in addition to the plays and law reports mentioned, wrote and published the following works:

1. 'The Algerine Captive, or The Life and Adventures of Doctor Updike Underhill, six years a prisoner among the Algerines.' 2 vols. Walpole, N. H., 1797.

2. 'Moral Tales for American Youths.' Boston, 1800.

3. 'The Yankey in London; a series of Letters written by an American Youth during nine months' residence in the City of London.' New-York, 1809.

He also contributed to a number of newspapers of his period, and a collection of his contributions (with those of Joseph Dennie) were published in a volume, at Walpole, in 1801, entitled 'The Spirit of the Farmers' Museum and Lay Preachers' Gazette.'

[4] On October 16th, 1778, the Continental Congress passed the following resolution:

"Whereas, frequenting play-houses and theatrical entertainments has a fatal tendency to divest the minds of the people from a due attention to the means necessary to the defence of their Country and preservation of their liberties;

"Resolved, That any person holding an office under the United States who shall act, promote, encourage or attend such play, shall be deemed unworthy to hold such office, and shall be accordingly dismissed."

T. J. McK.

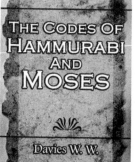

The Codes Of Hammurabi And Moses
W. W. Davies

The discovery of the Hammurabi Code is one of the greatest achievements of archaeology, and is of paramount interest, not only to the student of the Bible, but also to all those interested in ancient history...

Religion   ISBN: *1-59462-338-4*   Pages:132

QTY

MSRP $12.95

The Theory of Moral Sentiments
Adam Smith

This work from 1749. contains original theories of conscience amd moral judgment and it is the foundation for systemof morals.

Philosophy   ISBN: *1-59462-777-0*   Pages:536

QTY

MSRP $19.95

Jessica's First Prayer
Hesba Stretton

QTY

In a screened and secluded corner of one of the many railway-bridges which span the streets of London there could be seen a few years ago, from five o'clock every morning until half past eight, a tidily set-out coffee-stall, consisting of a trestle and board, upon which stood two large tin cans, with a small fire of charcoal burning under each so as to keep the coffee boiling during the early hours of the morning when the work-people were thronging into the city on their way to their daily toil...

Pages:84

Childrens   ISBN: *1-59462-373-2*   *MSRP $9.95*

My Life and Work
Henry Ford

QTY

Henry Ford revolutionized the world with his implementation of mass production for the Model T automobile. Gain valuable business insight into his life and work with his own auto-biography... "We have only started on our development of our country we have not as yet, with all our talk of wonderful progress, done more than scratch the surface. The progress has been wonderful enough but..."

Pages:300

Biographies/   ISBN: *1-59462-198-5*   *MSRP $21.95*

QTY

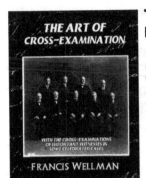

The Art of Cross-Examination
Francis Wellman

I presume it is the experience of every author, after his first book is published upon an important subject, to be almost overwhelmed with a wealth of ideas and illustrations which could readily have been included in his book, and which to his own mind, at least, seem to make a second edition inevitable. Such certainly was the case with me; and when the first edition had reached its sixth impression in five months, I rejoiced to learn that it seemed to my publishers that the book had met with a sufficiently favorable reception to justify a second and considerably enlarged edition. ..

Pages:412

Reference   **ISBN:** *1-59462-647-2*   *MSRP $19.95*

QTY

On the Duty of Civil Disobedience
Henry David Thoreau

Thoreau wrote his famous essay, On the Duty of Civil Disobedience, as a protest against an unjust but popular war and the immoral but popular institution of slave-owning. He did more than write—he declined to pay his taxes, and was hauled off to gaol in consequence. Who can say how much this refusal of his hastened the end of the war and of slavery ?

Pages:48

Law   **ISBN:** *1-59462-747-9*   *MSRP $7.45*

QTY

Dream Psychology Psychoanalysis for Beginners
Sigmund Freud

Sigmund Freud, born Sigismund Schlomo Freud (May 6, 1856 - September 23, 1939), was a Jewish-Austrian neurologist and psychiatrist who co-founded the psychoanalytic school of psychology. Freud is best known for his theories of the unconscious mind, especially involving the mechanism of repression; his redefinition of sexual desire as mobile and directed towards a wide variety of objects; and his therapeutic techniques, especially his understanding of transference in the therapeutic relationship and the presumed value of dreams as sources of insight into unconscious desires.

Pages:196

Psychology **ISBN:** *1-59462-905-6*   *MSRP $15.45*

QTY

The Miracle of Right Thought
Orison Swett Marden

Believe with all of your heart that you will do what you were made to do. When the mind has once formed the habit of holding cheerful, happy, prosperous pictures, it will not be easy to form the opposite habit. It does not matter how improbable or how far away this realization may see, or how dark the prospects may be, if we visualize them as best we can, as vividly as possible, hold tenaciously to them and vigorously struggle to attain them, they will gradually become actualized, realized in the life. But a desire, a longing without endeavor, a yearning abandoned or held indifferently will vanish without realization.

Pages:360

Self Help   **ISBN:** *1-59462-644-8*   *MSRP $25.45*

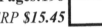

The Rosicrucian Cosmo-Conception Mystic Christianity by *Max Heindel* — ISBN: *1-59462-188-8* $38.95
The Rosicrucian Cosmo-conception is not dogmatic, neither does it appeal to any other authority than the reason of the student. It is: not controversial, but is: sent forth in the, hope that it may help to clear...
New Age/Religion Pages 646

Abandonment To Divine Providence by *Jean-Pierre de Caussade* — ISBN: *1-59462-228-0* $25.95
"The Rev. Jean Pierre de Caussade was one of the most remarkable spiritual writers of the Society of Jesus in France in the 18th Century. His death took place at Toulouse in 1751. His works have gone through many editions and have been republished...
Inspirational/Religion Pages 400

Mental Chemistry by *Charles Haanel* — ISBN: *1-59462-192-6* $23.95
Mental Chemistry allows the change of material conditions by combining and appropriately utilizing the power of the mind. Much like applied chemistry creates something new and unique out of careful combinations of chemicals the mastery of mental chemistry...
New Age Pages 354

The Letters of Robert Browning and Elizabeth Barret Barrett 1845-1846 vol II by *Robert Browning* and *Elizabeth Barrett*
Biographies Pages 596
ISBN: *1-59462-193-4* $35.95

Gleanings In Genesis (volume I) by *Arthur W. Pink* — ISBN: *1-59462-130-6* $27.45
Appropriately has Genesis been termed "the seed plot of the Bible" for in it we have, in germ form, almost all of the great doctrines which are afterwards fully developed in the books of Scripture which follow...
Religion/Inspirational Pages 420

The Master Key by *L. W. de Laurence* — ISBN: *1-59462-001-6* $30.95
In no branch of human knowledge has there been a more lively increase of the spirit of research during the past few years than in the study of Psychology, Concentration and Mental Discipline. The requests for authentic lessons in Thought Control, Mental Discipline and...
New Age/Business Pages 422

The Lesser Key Of Solomon Goetia by *L. W. de Laurence* — ISBN: *1-59462-092-X* $9.95
This translation of the first book of the "Lernegton" which is now for the first time made accessible to students of Talismanic Magic was done, after careful collation and edition, from numerous Ancient Manuscripts in Hebrew, Latin, and French...
New Age/Occult Pages 92

Rubaiyat Of Omar Khayyam by *Edward Fitzgerald* — ISBN:*1-59462-332-5* $13.95
Edward Fitzgerald, whom the world has already learned, in spite of his own efforts to remain within the shadow of anonymity, to look upon as one of the rarest poets of the century, was born at Bredfield, in Suffolk, on the 31st of March, 1809. He was the third son of John Purcell...
Music Pages 172

Ancient Law by *Henry Maine* — ISBN: *1-59462-128-4* $29.95
The chief object of the following pages is to indicate some of the earliest ideas of mankind, as they are reflected in Ancient Law, and to point out the relation of those ideas to modern thought.
Religion/History Pages 452

Far-Away Stories by *William J. Locke* — ISBN: *1-59462-129-2* $19.45
"Good wine needs no bush, but a collection of mixed vintages does. And this book is just such a collection. Some of the stories I do not want to remain buried for ever in the museum files of dead magazine-numbers an author's not unpardonable vanity..."
Fiction Pages 272

Life of David Crockett by *David Crockett* — ISBN: *1-59462-250-7* $27.45
"Colonel David Crockett was one of the most remarkable men of the times in which he lived. Born in humble life, but gifted with a strong will, an indomitable courage, and unremitting perseverance...
Biographies/New Age Pages 424

Lip-Reading by *Edward Nitchie* — ISBN: *1-59462-206-X* $25.95
Edward B. Nitchie, founder of the New York School for the Hard of Hearing, now the Nitchie School of Lip-Reading, Inc, wrote "LIP-READING Principles and Practice". The development and perfecting of this meritorious work on lip-reading was an undertaking...
How-to Pages 400

A Handbook of Suggestive Therapeutics, Applied Hypnotism, Psychic Science by *Henry Munro* — ISBN: *1-59462-214-0* $24.95
Health/New Age/Health/Self-help Pages 376

A Doll's House: and Two Other Plays by *Henrik Ibsen* — ISBN: *1-59462-112-8* $19.95
Henrik Ibsen created this classic when in revolutionary 1848 Rome. Introducing some striking concepts in playwriting for the realist genre, this play has been studied the world over.
Fiction/Classics/Plays 308

The Light of Asia by *sir Edwin Arnold* — ISBN: *1-59462-204-3* $13.95
In this poetic masterpiece, Edwin Arnold describes the life and teachings of Buddha. The man who was to become known as Buddha to the world was born as Prince Gautama of India but he rejected the worldly riches and abandoned the reigns of power when...
Religion/History/Biographies Pages 170

The Complete Works of Guy de Maupassant by *Guy de Maupassant* — ISBN: *1-59462-157-8* $16.95
"For days and days, nights and nights, I had dreamed of that first kiss which was to consecrate our engagement, and I knew not on what spot I should put my lips..."
Fiction/Classics Pages 240

The Art of Cross-Examination by *Francis L. Wellman* — ISBN: *1-59462-309-0* $26.95
Written by a renowned trial lawyer, Wellman imparts his experience and uses case studies to explain how to use psychology to extract desired information through questioning.
How-to/Science/Reference Pages 408

Answered or Unanswered? by *Louisa Vaughan* — ISBN: *1-59462-248-5* $10.95
Miracles of Faith in China
Religion Pages 112

The Edinburgh Lectures on Mental Science (1909) by *Thomas* — ISBN: *1-59462-008-3* $11.95
This book contains the substance of a course of lectures recently given by the writer in the Queen Street Hall, Edinburgh. Its purpose is to indicate the Natural Principles governing the relation between Mental Action and Material Conditions...
New Age/Psychology Pages 148

Ayesha by *H. Rider Haggard* — ISBN: *1-59462-301-5* $24.95
Verily and indeed it is the unexpected that happens! Probably if there was one person upon the earth from whom the Editor of this, and of a certain previous history, did not expect to hear again...
Classics Pages 380

Ayala's Angel by *Anthony Trollope* — ISBN: *1-59462-352-X* $29.95
The two girls were both pretty, but Lucy who was twenty-one who supposed to be simple and comparatively unattractive, whereas Ayala was credited, as her Bombwhat romantic name might show, with poetic charm and a taste for romance. Ayala when her father died was nineteen...
Fiction Pages 484

The American Commonwealth by *James Bryce* — ISBN: *1-59462-286-8* $34.45
An interpretation of American democratic political theory. It examines political mechanics and society from the perspective of Scotsman James Bryce
Politics Pages 572

Stories of the Pilgrims by *Margaret P. Pumphrey* — ISBN: *1-59462-116-0* $17.95
This book explores pilgrims religious oppression in England as well as their escape to Holland and eventual crossing to America on the Mayflower, and their early days in New England...
History Pages 268

QTY

The Fasting Cure *by Sinclair Upton*   ISBN: *1-59462-222-1* **$13.95**

In the Cosmopolitan Magazine for May, 1910, and in the Contemporary Review (London) for April, 1910, I published an article dealing with my experiences in fasting. I have written a great many magazine articles, but never one which attracted so much attention... New Age/Self Help/Health Pages 164

☐

Hebrew Astrology *by Sepharial*   ISBN: *1-59462-308-2* **$13.45**

In these days of advanced thinking it is a matter of common observation that we have left many of the old landmarks behind and that we are now pressing forward to greater heights and to a wider horizon than that which represented the mind-content of our progenitors... Astrology Pages 144

☐

Thought Vibration or The Law of Attraction in the Thought World   ISBN: *1-59462-127-6* **$12.95**

by William Walker Atkinson   *Psychology/Religion Pages 144*

☐

Optimism *by Helen Keller*   ISBN: *1-59462-108-X* **$15.95**

Helen Keller was blind, deaf, and mute since 19 months old, yet famously learned how to overcome these handicaps, communicate with the world, and spread her lectures promoting optimism. An inspiring read for everyone... Biographies/Inspirational Pages 84

☐

Sara Crewe *by Frances Burnett*   ISBN: *1-59462-360-0* **$9.45**

In the first place, Miss Minchin lived in London. Her home was a large, dull, tall one, in a large, dull square, where all the houses were alike, and all the sparrows were alike, and where all the door-knockers made the same heavy sound... Childrens/Classic Pages 88

☐

The Autobiography of Benjamin Franklin *by Benjamin Franklin*   ISBN: *1-59462-135-7* **$24.95**

The Autobiography of Benjamin Franklin has probably been more extensively read than any other American historical work, and no other book of its kind has had such ups and downs of fortune. Franklin lived for many years in England, where he was agent... Biographies/History Pages 332

☐

Name	
Email	
Telephone	
Address	
City, State ZIP	

☐ **Credit Card**   ☐ **Check / Money Order**

Credit Card Number	
Expiration Date	
Signature	

Please Mail to: Book Jungle
PO Box 2226
Champaign, IL 61825
or Fax to: 630-214-0564

ORDERING INFORMATION

web: *www.bookjungle.com*
email: *sales@bookjungle.com*
fax: *630-214-0564*
mail: *Book Jungle PO Box 2226 Champaign, IL 61825*
or PayPal *to sales@bookjungle.com*

Please contact us for bulk discounts

DIRECT-ORDER TERMS

**20% Discount if You Order
Two or More Books**
Free Domestic Shipping!
Accepted: Master Card, Visa,
Discover, American Express

CPSIA information can be obtained at www.ICGtesting.com
Printed in the USA
LVOW02s2052220714

395503LV00011BA/748/P

9 781438 527321